Federal Intervention in
the Mortgage Markets
An Analysis

Research for Business Decisions, No. 64

Richard N. Farmer, Series Editor

Professor of International Business
Indiana University

Other Titles in This Series

Federal Intervention in the Mortgage Markets
An Analysis

by
Douglas Hearth

UMI RESEARCH PRESS
Ann Arbor, Michigan

Produced and distributed by
UMI Research Press
an imprint of
University Microfilms International
Ann Arbor, Michigan 48106

Library of Congress Cataloging in Publication Data

Hearth, Douglas.
   Federal intervention in the mortgage markets.

   (Research for business decisions ; no. 64)
   Revision of author's thesis (Ph.D.)–University of
Iowa, 1981.
   Bibliography: p.
   Includes index.
   1. Mortgage loans–Government policy–United States.
2. Interest rates–United States. I. Title. II. Series.

HG2040.5.U5H4   1983   332.7'2   83-17880
ISBN 0-8357-1484-5

Contents

List of Tables

List of Figures

1

Introduction

Purpose

A growing body of empirical literature suggests that federal policies designed to increase and stabilize the availability of residential mortgage credit have little, if any, long term effect. The purpose of this study is to examine one possible cause of this long term ineffectiveness. Specifically, this study will examine the impact of federal mortgage agency activity on the structure of market interest rates. It will also examine the portfolio behavior of financial institutions in response to changes in interest rates.

The Residential Mortgage Market

At the outset, it will be useful to briefly outline the structure of the residential mortgage market in the United States. Essentially there are several lenders of mortgage funds (savings and loans, mutual savings banks, commercial banks, life insurance companies, other private lenders, and several federal credit agencies) and one principal borrower (households).

The suppliers of mortgages acquire funds through a variety of means. Savings and loans (SLAs), mutual savings banks (MSBs), and commercial banks (CBs) acquire funds primarily through the issuance of non-marketable deposits to the public and by selling short term securities (mainly certificates of deposit). In addition all three may borrow funds from the appropriate governmental agency (the Federal Home Loan Bank for SLAs and MSBs, and Federal Reserve for CBs). Life insurance companies (LICs) acquire funds in the form of life insurance reserves by selling insurance policies to the public. Other private mortgage lenders, such as finance companies, raise funds by selling securities and by borrowing from banks. The federal credit agencies raise funds exclusively by selling securities.

An additional participant in the mortgage market is the mortgage banker. While not technically a supplier of mortgage funds, the mortgage banker nonetheless plays an important role in the mortgage market. A mortgage banker is an individual or a firm which locates prospective borrowers, completes necessary documents and frequently disburses its own, or borrowed funds to complete a real estate transaction. Usually the mortgage banker sells the loan to a financial institution.[1] After the sale, the mortgage banker continues to service the loan. In recent years, mortgage bankers have originated approximately one-fifth of the dollar value of all residential mortgages.

It is important to distinguish between discretionary and non-discretionary lenders. SLAs are essentially non-discretionary lenders; they channel most of their funds into mortgages.[2] Discretionary mortgage lenders will shift their portfolios among mortgages, other consumer loans and securities as market conditions change. In recent years, MSBs, CBs and LICs may all be classified as discretionary mortgage lenders. Federal credit agencies may be viewed as being non-discretionary lenders since they exist to channel the vast majority of their funds into the mortgage market.

Table 1 illustrates the changes which have occurred since 1950 in the distribution of outstanding mortgage debt among the various lenders. Two major trends are evident from these data. One, the non-discretionary lenders now hold 59.7% of outstanding mortgage debt compared to 32.3% in 1950 and 44.0% in 1960. Two, the relative importance of federal and related agencies, as mortgage lenders, has risen dramatically since 1970.

Relationship Between Housing Construction Activity and the Mortgage Market

Since the end of World War II, housing construction activity has shown significant cyclical fluctuations, increasing rapidly during periods of economic growth and falling substantially during recessions. Rosen and Kearl (1974) suggest that residential construction has served as a "sponge" for the

Table 1.   Distribution of Outstanding
One to Four Family Residential Mortgage Debts,
by Holder, from 1950 to 1982

	1950	1960	1970	1975	1982
Savings and loans	29.0%	39.0%	41.8%	45.6%	36.3%
Mutual savings banks	9.5	14.5	14.1	10.2	5.8
Commercial banks	21.0	13.5	14.2	15.7	16.0
Life Insurance companies	18.8	17.5	9.0	3.6	1.5
Federal and related agencies	3.3	5.0	8.3	13.8	23.4
Individuals and others	18.4	10.4	12.5	11.1	17.0

Source: *Federal Reserve Bulletin*, various issues.

business cycle, releasing factors of production in periods of strong growth and absorbing them in recessions.

Guttentag (1961) and Alberts (1962) were among the first to argue the importance of the cost and availability of mortgage credit to housing construction activity. Conditions in the mortgage market may be seen as exerting three influences on residential construction activity. The first of these views residential mortgages as residual investments for financial institutions. During periods of tight credit, the inflow of funds to these institutions decreases and thus there is less money available for residual investments.

Secondly, a reduction in the inflow of funds to financial institutions puts upward pressure on the mortgage rate, depressing demand for mortgage funds. A reduction on either the amount of mortgage credit demanded or supplied will be viewed by builders as a signal to slow down their new construction activity.

Finally, a third influence directly affects the willingness of a financial institution to make mortgage commitments. A decline in the inflow of funds would most likely cause the number of new commitments to decrease.

A number of empirical studies have attempted to determine the impact of credit availability and mortgage terms on housing activity. Most construct models designed to explain the post-war building cycle.[3] While specific methodology and conclusions differ from study to study, the general conclusion reached by most is that both the cost and the availability of mortgage credit are important determinants of short run fluctuations in housing activity. It should be noted that this conclusion is not universally accepted.[4]

Role of the Federal Government

The federal government has long viewed housing as a key industry and it has been manipulated to achieve a variety of social and economic goals. In addition, federal policies have been successful, in the past, at achieving social goals within a housing context. For example, Rosen and Rosen (1980) estimate that at least 25% of the increase in the proportion of home ownership since 1947 is a direct result of changes in federal tax policy.

The origins of federal policies designed to increase and stabilize the availability of mortgage credit may be traced back to the Depression. Since the mid-nineteen-thirties, the size and scope of these policies, and the agencies they have created, have greatly expanded. Much of the expansion has occurred when there has been noticeable weakening in the housing and mortgage markets. For example, Cook (1974) argues that the 1968 Housing and Urban Development Act and 1970 Emergency Home Finance Act were, in part, responses to sluggish construction activity and tight credit conditions which occurred in 1966–1967 and 1969–1970. Both acts significantly expanded the role of the federal government in the home finance area.

Two types of activities by federal and related agencies are the primary policy instruments used to increase and stabilize mortgage credit availability. The first is advances to member financial institutions (primarily savings and loans) by the Federal Home Loan Bank (FHLB). Advances are designed to ease liquidity problems caused by disintermediation. Advances are short term sources of funds and must be repaid to the FHLB with interest. Since mortgages are the primary asset of a savings and loan, easing short term liquidity problems should help maintain the flow of mortgage loans and commitments even in a period of rising interest rates and tight credit.

Second is the secondary mortgage market operations of three Federally Sponsored Credit Agencies (FSCA): the Federal National Mortgage Association, the Government National Mortgage Association and the Federal Home Loan Mortgage Corporation.[5] FSCAs purchase mortgages from primary lenders (e.g., savings and loans) and then hold the mortgages in their portfolios or resell them to other investors. In theory, FSCA activities will allow primary lenders to increase their loan and commitment volume. In addition, FSCA mortgage purchases may be seen as an alternative source of funds for primary lenders; useful in periods when the inflow of savings from the public slows.

An examination of the past behavior of the federal mortgage agencies

Table 2.   Summary of Federal Mortgage Agency Activity:
1960–1982 (Billions of Dollars)

Year End	Outstanding Federal Home Loan Bank Advances	Mortgage Debt Held by Federal and Related Agencies	
		Total Mortgage Portfolios	Mortgage Pools
1960	1,979	11,200	—
1965	5,985	12,400	—
1970	10,488	32,200	452
1975	17,524	66,891	34,138
1976	15,708	66,753	49,801
1977	19,945	70,175	70,202
1978	31,990	81,739	88,633
1979	40,441	97,084	119,278
1980	47,045	114,300	142,258
1981	62,794	126,112	162,990
1982	63,861	139,291	214,430

Sources: *Federal Reserve Bulletin*, various issues and *Federal Home Loan Bank Board Journal*, various issues.

indicates that, in general, they have responded in a countercyclical manner to conditions in the housing and mortgage markets. For example, historically a decline in the flow of funds to financial institutions has corresponded with increases in FHLB advance and FSCA purchase activity and vice versa.

Also evident from the data is the fact that the level of agency activity has increased in recent years. Table 2 summarizes FHLB and FSCA activity since 1960. Outstanding FHLB advances increased between 1960 and 1975 at an annual rate of approximately 15%. However between 1975 and 1982, the annual rate of growth of outstanding FHLB advances exceeded 20%.

Likewise the level of FSCA activity has accelerated in recent years. FSCA mortgage portfolios (mortgages actually held by FSCAs) grew at an annual rate of 11.2% between 1960 and 1970; and portfolios grew at an annual rate of 13.0% between 1970 and 1982. FSCA mortgage pools (mortgages backed by GNMA or FHLMC securities) grew at a much faster rate than did FSCA portfolios between 1975 and 1982. The annual rate of growth exceeded 30% between 1975 and 1982.

Evaluation of Federal Mortgage Policy

Numerous attempts have been made to evaluate the effectiveness of federal efforts designed to increase and stabilize the availability of mortgage credit. Early studies (most completed between 1968 and 1973) treat FSCA and FHLB activities as exogenous variables (i.e., independent). In most cases, these studies attempt to determine the impact of FHLB and FSCA activities on the supply of mortgage credit and/or the level of housing construction activity.

More recent studies have recognized that FHLB and FSCA activities are not exogenous to the mortgage and housing markets. Rather they are endogenous; agency activities respond to conditions in the markets. Many of these studies model FSCA and FHLB behavior in response to changing market conditions, drawing inferences about their ability to achieve policy objectives.

It is difficult to generalize about conclusions reached by existing empirical studies. Nevertheless, one consistent theme seems to be emerging from the most recent work: FHLB advances and/or FSCA secondary market operations have essentially no effect on the mortgage or housing markets over extended periods (beyond about a year). However, agency actions may have significant short run impacts.[6]

The crux of the argument that FHLB and FSCA activities have no effect, in the long run, on either the housing or mortgage markets is based upon the notion that their actions (which are basically expansionary) lead to offsetting reactions by private market participants. These reactions are caused by changes in market interest rate patterns which are a direct or indirect result of agency activities.

Cook (1974) found evidence which suggests agency activity has put upward pressure on the government bond rate while at the same time depressing the mortgage rate. It is these two interest rate changes, Cook argues, which are primarily responsible for three reactions by private market participants which dilute the expansionary effects of agency activities. Cook refers to these reactions as "leakages" of funds.

The first leakage says that households will likely substitute government securities for savings deposits at financial institutions, reducing the flow of funds to the financial institutions. This leakage is a result of a widening in the spread between the government bond rate and the rate paid on savings deposits. Second, a decline in the mortgage rate relative to other consumer loan rates might induce households to substitute mortgage debt for owner's equity. Households would increase their relative use of mortgage debt, but not their investment in housing. Third, the spread between the government bond rate and the mortgage rate would appear to widen as a consequence of FHLB and FSCA activities; government bonds would become more attractive investments relative to mortgages. Since some financial institutions (especially discretionary mortgage lenders) regard government bonds and mortgages as essentially substitutes, an increase in the spread would likely lead to portfolio adjustments by these institutions.

The apparent dichotomy in recent empirical evidence between short term and long term effectiveness of FHLB and FSCA activities, mentioned earlier, may be explained within the context of Cook's three leakages. For example, Cook presents some evidence that federal agencies have responded rapidly to changing mortgage and housing market conditions. On the other hand, discretionary private lenders may react to changing market conditions much slower. Therefore, even if mortgages and government bonds are close substitutes in these lenders' portfolios, the third leakage might be small in the short run. As a result, FSCA and FHLB actions may have a significant short term impact, yet have no significant long term impact.

Unanswered Questions

Three major questions may be raised concerning the preceding discussion. First, how rapidly do the federal agencies respond to changes in housing and mortgage market conditions? Does the timing of FHLB/FSCA actions optimize their short term effectiveness? Second, how does federal agency activity affect the structure of market interest rates? Third, how significant are Cook's three leakages? If, for example, some private mortgage lenders react to changes in market interest rates by making portfolio adjustments, how severe are these reactions and how long do they take? All three questions are important to any overall evaluation of the effectiveness of federal mortgage policy. In these instances, the existing literature is not complete. This study will attempt to partly fill these voids.

This study will empirically investigate the possible impact of federal mortgage agency activity on the structure of market interest rates. Specifically, it will examine whether, as a consequence of federal mortgage agency activity, mortgages become less attractive investments (on a yield basis) vis-à-vis other long term financial assets (corporate bonds, treasury bonds, etc.). This study will also seek to determine whether changes in yield spreads between mortgages and other financial assets lead to portfolio adjustments by mortgage lenders diminishing the effectiveness of FHLB and FSCA activities.

Preview of Subsequent Chapters

Functions of a brief history of the Federal Home Loan Bank and the three Federally Sponsored Credit Agencies will be discussed in the next chapter. A review of the relevant literatures will follow in chapter 3. Chapters 4, 5 and 6 will be devoted to methodology, hypotheses and empirical results. The concluding chapter will be devoted to a discussion of public policy implications and avenues for further research.

2

The Federal Mortgage Agencies
History and Analysis

Introduction

Chapter 2 will discuss the origins and development of the four federal mortgage agencies and the programs they administer. Included will be a discussion of each agency's history, relevant legislation and current operations. For purposes of organization, this chapter will be divided by agency.

Federal Home Loan Bank Board

Overview

The Federal Home Loan Bank Board (FHLBB) is the oldest of the federal mortgage credit agencies. It is responsible for administering the Federal Home Loan Bank System (which includes 12 regional FHLB Banks and member financial institutions), the Federal Savings and Loan Insurance Corporation (FSLIC) and the Federal Home Loan Mortgage Corporation (FHLMC). This section will concentrate primarily on the FHLB system; the FHLMC will be discussed specifically in a later section.

Statutory Origins The Federal Home Loan Bank System was established by three pieces of Depression era legislation. The first, and most important, was the 1932 Federal Home Loan Bank Act (47 Stat. 725). This act, established the regional Banks under the supervision of the FHLB Board. Its primary purpose was to provide a central credit facility to supplement the resources of financial institutions engaged in making home loans. This act, therefore, represented the first major attempt by the federal government to increase and stabilize the availability of mortgage credit. The 1932 act was a response to serious deterioration in the home finance area brought about by the Depression. For example, in the 1930s more than 1,700 savings and loans, the primary source of home mortgage money, failed.[1]

The 1932 act was followed by two other pieces of legislation. The 1933 Home Owner's Loan Act (48 Stat. 128), which authorized creation, under the FHLBB, of a system of federally chartered and supervised savings and loan associations, and the 1934 National Housing Act (48 Stat. 1255) which established the Federal Savings and Loan Insurance Corporation. Although widely amended since the mid-thirties, these acts nonetheless still form the primary statutory basis of the modern FHLB System.[2]

System Structure   The FHLB System is organized in much the same way the Federal Reserve System is organized. The Bank Board, which consists of three members, governs and regulates the entire system. It sets general policy regarding the terms and conditions on the FHLB advances, the chartering of federal SLAs, the maintenance of minimum liquidity requirements for members and so forth.

All federally chartered SLAs are required by law to belong to the System. Membership is voluntary for qualified state chartered SLAs, mutual savings banks and life insurance companies. As of March 31, 1981, 4,212 financial institutions belonged to the System. Of that number 4,062 were SLAs, 148 were mutual savings banks and two were insurance companies.[3]

The nation is divided into 12 regions or districts, each with its own regional Bank. The Banks are responsible for carrying out the functions of the System in its dealings with member institutions. Banks hold member deposits and loan funds, called advances, to them. Banks have the power to set maturities, interest rates and other terms and conditions on these advances within general policy guidelines set down by the FHLB Board.

Each regional Bank is owned by their members, who appoint several members of the board of directors (the others are appointed by the Bank Board). Since the System was created, the amount of policy discretion given the Banks by the Board has varied. Marvell (1969) suggests that the relationship between the Banks and the FHLB Board has been the largest source of conflict within the System. Member institutions have pushed for greater autonomy for the Banks which is not surprising since they exert more influence on the Banks than they do on the Board.

Sources of Funds   The FHLB Board is an independent federal agency and as such receives no direct congressional appropriations. The Bank Board's major sources of funds are: examination fees, assessments on the regional Banks and assessments on the FSLIC. The Board's chief expense is employee compensation.[4]

Since the Banks actually provide advances to members, they raise substantially more funds. The largest single source of funds for the Banks comes from the sale of FHLB System consolidated obligations. These obligations are approved and marketed by the Bank Board as system-wide obligations. FHLB securities have much the same institutional status as treasury securities: both may be used as collateral for Federal Reserve loans and discounts, both are exempt from SEC registration, both are legal investments for federally chartered institutions, and so forth. However, two important differences between FHLB and treasury securities exist. First, like all federal agency securities, FHLB securities are not backed by the full faith and credit of the United States Government and thus, in theory, carry some default risk. It is unlikely, however, that many investors would seriously entertain the notion that Congress would allow a federal agency to default. Second, FHLB borrowings are off-budget and thus are not subject to federal debt ceilings.[5]

In recent years, the FHLB System has tapped the money and capital markets for large amounts of funds; excluding FHLMC borrowings $24.9 billion in 1980.[6] At the end of 1982 outstanding debt obligations totaled $61.4 billion, an increase of over 280 percent since 1970.[7]

Regional Banks have several other sources of funds available to them. These include: deposits by member institutions, sale of capital stock (to new and existing members) and income derived from advances and short term investments (usually treasury bills). The major uses of funds are net advances (new advances minus repayments) and the purchase of short term securities. The 1980 balance sheet and 1980 sources and uses of funds statement for the Banks are presented in table 3.

FHLB Advances

Excluding programs administered by the Mortgage Corporation, no other program or policy of the FHLB Board has as much potential impact on the availability of mortgage credit as FHLB advances.[8] In 1981 FHLB Banks made over $53 billion in advances to member and non-member institutions.[9]

Terms and Conditions   Terms and conditions on advances are set at three levels. First, the Federal Home Loan Bank Act, and subsequent legislation, set only very general guidelines concerning advances. Second, the FHLB Board sets general policy outlining terms and conditions on advances. Third, regional Banks set their own specific policies within the frameworks established by the 1932 Act and the Bank Board. At times regional Banks have been given wide discretion to set specific terms and conditions on advances, and at times the Board has given the banks little, if any discretion. As a result, substantial variation between regions has existed.

There are five terms and conditions on advances which are worthy of discussion: the interest rate charged borrowers, acceptable collateral, length

Table 3.   1979 & 1980 Common Size
Financial Statements for FHLB Banks

Balance Sheet

Assets	1980	1979
Cash	.5%	.5%
Marketable Securities	8.0	8.0
Outstanding Advances	90.1	90.1
Other Assets	1.4	1.4
Liabilities & Capital		
Deposits	18.7%	20.2%
Consolidated Obligations	68.6	65.4
Other Liabilities	1.6	1.3
Capital Stock	9.5	11.1
Retained Earnings	1.6	2.0

Sources and Uses of Funds

Sources		
From Operations	1.6%	2.3%
Sale of Obligations	90.6	78.4
Deposits	3.0	13.1
Sales of Capital Stock	1.4	3.8
Other Sources	3.4	2.4
Uses		
Net Increase in Advances	25.9%	39.5%
Repayment of Obligations	67.8	57.6
Stock Redemption	2.1	—
Increase in Short Term Investments	2.3	1.2
Cash Dividends	1.1	1.0
Other Uses	.8	.8

Source: *FHLBB Annual Report*, 1980, pp. 80–84.

of time funds may be borrowed, amount one institution may borrow and the use of advances.

The 1932 Act states: "such advances shall be made . . . bearing such rate of interest the board may approve or determine" (Section 10, paragraph 4c). Bank Board regulations are equally vague stating the rate of interest on advances shall be set "within the range established by the Board" (Section 525.3, FHLBB Regulations). After examining past and current advance practices, it appears that the following factors are taken into account by the Board and Banks when setting advance rates: financial condition of borrowers, cost of FHLB obligations, and the cost of other sources of funds (e.g., deposits) to borrowers. If, for example, the rate paid on savings deposits exceeded the cost of advances, borrowers would make money by obtaining advances from the Banks rather than attracting new savings. As a result, the advance rate has usually exceeded savings account rates; however, at times since 1970 the advance rate has been well below the cost of FHLB obligations.[10]

Regional Banks are permitted to make both secured and unsecured advances. In general advances may be secured by mortgages, government securities and other securities. Rules and regulations concerning collateral are rather complicated. For example, usually the value of collateral must exceed the amount of the advance.[11] Secured advances are the most common type today. As Marvell (1969) points out, the Banks have been stressing secured advances because collateral enhances the financial position of Banks, making FHLB obligations more marketable.

The amount any one institution may borrow is limited by both statute and by FHLB regulation. In December 1979 Congress amended the 1932 Act increasing the amount an institution could borrow from 12 times to 20 times the amount of Bank Capital Stock the institution held. In addition, Section 525.1 of FHLBB Regulation limits advances to 50 percent of net assets or 50 percent of deposits. However, few institutions, if any, have ever approached the maximum. At the end of 1980, outstanding advances equaled less than 10 percent of savings deposits and less than eight percent of net assets.[12]

Up until 1966 the maturity of advances varied across the country; some banks only allowed one-year advances while others allowed advances of up to ten years (the statutory limit). In 1966, the Bank Board decided to limit all advances to one year. Members wishing to borrow funds in excess of one year were required to renew advances annually. The purpose of this restriction was to give banks more control over advance volume and keep advance rates in line with Bank Board policy. This policy was gradually liberalized until, in 1977, the Board returned to the Banks almost total discretion to set advance maturities up to ten years.

The 1932 Act did not specify what advances could be used for, however, there is little doubt that Congress intended advances to increase the supply of mortgage credit and also stabilize the supply by covering savings withdrawals. For years, in fact, FHLBB regulations specified two types of advances: expansion (designed to allow members to increase their mortgage portfolios) and liquidity (designed to cover disintermediation). The Bank Board abolished this distinction in 1973, and current policy on the use of advances is much more general; advances should be used to meet clear needs for funds, not to take advantage of rate differentials (Section 531.1, FHLBB Regulations).

Advance Activity   Table 4 shows the relationship between advance activity (net change in outstanding advances) and savings flows (net savings inflows to savings and loan associations) from 1960 to 1981. The data clearly suggest that most FHLB borrowers consider advances to be a substitute for savings deposits. This gives rise to the counter-cyclical relationship.

The most recent years of disintermediation (1974 and 1981), when savings inflows slowed substantially, corresponded with major increases in outstanding advances; they increased by 43.9 percent in 1974 and 33.5 percent in 1981. On the other hand, in 1976 savings deposits grew by over 17 percent while outstanding advances fell by approximately 11 percent.[13]

Despite this basically counter-cyclical relationship, outstanding advances increased by over 498 percent from 1970 to 1981 while, at the same time, savings deposits grew by 259 percent and net assets (of savings and loans) grew by 277 percent. As a result, the ratio of outstanding advances to savings deposits increased from 7.4 percent to 12.0 percent between 1970 and 1981. Likewise the ratio of outstanding advances to net assets increased from 6.1 percent in 1970 to 9.5 percent in 1981. While both ratios are still well below statutory and regulatory limits, these increases have generated concern in both the Bank Board and Congress and are an indication of the current financial condition of many of the nation's thrift institutions.[14]

The discretion given regional Banks recently to set lending policies, coupled with regional differences in size, mortgage demand, savings flows, and so forth have produced significant differences in advance activity among the 12 districts. Table 5 provides some evidence of this. In 1979, 90 percent of eligible institutions in district 12 were regular borrowers while only 50 percent of eligible institutions in district 2 were regular borrowers. Between 1979 and 1980 outstanding advances increased by 17 percent nationwide; in district 7 they fell by over 4 percent while in district 11 they rose by almost 40 percent. In 1978, the average cost of advances was 8.48 percent, ranging from a high of 9.09 percent in district three to a low of 7.80 percent in district 10.

Special Advance Programs   Since 1970, the FHLB Board has authorized several special advance programs aimed at correcting perceived weaknesses in the housing and home finance areas. These programs usually involve offering FHLB borrowers advances at reduced rates provided the funds are used for specific purposes.

In April 1970 the Bank Board created the Specially Priced Advance Program, while offered advances at "a reduced rate provided they (FHLB borrowers) converted their outstanding borrowings into advances repayable before the end of one year."[15] The purpose of the program was to give mortgage lenders an incentive to use new deposits to make mortgage loans,

Table 4. Net Savings Inflows and Net FHLB Advance Activity (Millions of Dollars)

Year	Net Savings Inflows	Net Advances
1960	7,559	−154
1965	8,513	672
1966	3,615	938
1967	10,649	−2,549
1968	7,478	873
1969	4,079	4,030
1970	11,018	1,326
1971	27,974	−2,678
1972	32,663	42
1973	20,237	7,168
1974	16,068	6,657
1975	42,806	−3,957
1976	50,585	−1,983
1977	51,016	4,311
1978	44,864	12,497
1979	39,304	9,168
1980	41,417	7,125
1981	13,425	15,749

Source *FHLBB Annual Report*, 1960–1981.

Table 5. Regional Differences in FHLB Advance Activity

Region		Percent Regular Borrowers	1979–1980		1978
			% Δ in Savings	% Δ in Advances	Average Rate
1	Boston	74%	86.9%	1.8%	8.47%
2	New York	50	24.6	23.3	8.61
3	Pittsburgh	58	69.3	0.8	9.09
4	Atlanta	68	13.5	18.7	8.52
5	Cincinnati	60	15.5	6.0	8.26
6	Indianapolis	57	27.4	2.9	8.41
7	Chicago	65	22.8	−4.4	8.40
8	Des Moines	77	22.6	7.5	8.35
9	Little Rock	62	24.9	8.1	8.44
10	Topeka	81	17.7	11.3	7.80
11	San Francisco	76	−38.3	39.6	8.89
12	Seattle	90	−15.0	11.3	8.54
	United States	65	5.3	17.0	8.48

Source: *FHLBB Journal*, various issues.

rather than use the funds to repay existing advances. Approximately $9 billion in specially priced advances were authorized, 97 percent of which ($8.7 billion) were committed by the end of 1970.[16]

Faced with serious disintermediation and a sharp reduction in mortgage market activity, the Board created another special advance program in May 1974. It authorized $4 billion in advances with a maturity of five years at an interest rate 50 basis points below the rate on corresponding regular advances. By the end of 1974, $3.5 billion of these advances had been made.[17]

In an attempt to stimulate the revitalization of older communities, the Bank Board (in cooperation with the Department of Housing and Urban Development) created in June 1978 a community investment fund (CIF). Mortgage lenders willing to participate in community revitalization projects were offered advances are lower than market rates. The program made available $2 billion per year (for five years) in CIF advances. At the end of 1980, outstanding CIF advances approached $5 billion.[18]

In response to the severe drop in the financial condition of many savings and loan associations, the Bank Board created a special advance program (called the Targeted Advance Program, or TAP) in 1980. SLAs which satisfied two need criteria were offered advances at an interest rate 250 basis points below market. One hundred twenty-one million dollars in TAP advances were made in 1980.[19]

Federal National Mortgage Association

The Federal National Mortgage Association (often referred to as Fannie Mae) is the oldest and largest of the three federally sponsored secondary mortgage market agencies. Fannie Mae exists to provide an interregional mortgage market by taking funds from capital surplus regions and investing them in capital deficient areas, provide a source of liquidity for primary mortgage lenders, which gives these lenders flexibility in adjusting their mortgage portfolios, and tap additional sources of capital in order to increase the availability of mortgage credit.

History

Creation and Early Development: 1933-1954   The first organization to bear the name Federal National Mortgage Association was established in 1938. Its creation represented a continuation of a process first begun in 1933 designed to improve the liquidity of mortgages by creating a secondary mortgage market. Overcoming liquidity problems represented one aspect of federal policy designed to support the home finance industry in the face of the Depression. The other aspect was the establishment of the Federal Home Loan Bank System.

Prior to 1933, few mortgage loans were fully amortized—most were five to ten years balloon loans. In addition, specific terms and lending procedures varied widely across the country. Faced wth these facts as well as a record number of foreclosures, Congress created the Home Owner's Loan Corporation in 1933. It was authorized to re-finance existing indebtedness with fully amortized loans. Thus, it was the first step toward creating a more uniform mortgage instrument.

The next step was taken in 1934 with the passage of the National Housing Act. This Act created the Federal Housing Administration (FHA). FHA instituted mortgage insurance and standardized nationwide underwriting procedures. Both were essential if a viable secondary mortgage market was to be established.

The National Housing Act also provided for the establishment of privately financed national mortgage associations to be chartered by FHA. These associations, it was hoped, would provide an indirect source of credit to the mortgage market, and would facilitate the flow of funds from capital surplus regions to capital deficient regions. By and large, the associations were unable to obtain adequate private financing and most failed. FHA's authority to charter mortgage associations was repealed in 1948.

It thus became apparent that without some direct public financing the secondary mortgage market could not adequately develop. Therefore, Congress added a section to the Reconstruction Finance Corporation Act (49 Stat. 1) establishing the RFC Mortgage Company. It was authorized to purchase existing FHA insured loans as well as act as a lender of last resort.

The volume of mortgage purchases needed in the mid-nineteen thirties soon outstripped the capabilities and capacity of the RFC Mortgage Company. As a result, in 1938, by executive order, President Roosevelt had a new mortgage association organized. Initially called the National Mortgage Association of Washington, it was soon renamed the Federal National Mortgage Association.

Initially, FNMA was placed under the direct supervision of the RFC, which provided FNMA's initial funding. At first, Fannie Mae was limited to purchasing FHA insured mortgages on homes constructed after 1936. In 1944, the Serviceman's Readjustment Act (58 Stat. 284) was passed. This Act expanded mortgage loan guarantees to servicemen under the Veterans Administration. It was designed to encourage private lending, but also gave FNMA the authority to purchase VA guaranteed mortgages starting in 1948. In 1950, Congress transferred Fannie Mae to the Housing and Home Finance Administration (now the Department of Housing and Urban Development—HUD) and soon abolished the RFC.

1954 to 1968   Congress, as well as much of the home finance industry, began to believe that eventually the entire secondary market system should be privately financed. This belief led to Title II of the 1954 Housing Act (68 Stat. 615).

The 1954 Act chartered FNMA as a quasi-private corporation partly owned by the federal government and partly owner by user financial institutions. Fannie Mae did, however, remain part of HHFA.

Under the reorganization, Fannie Mae was assigned three functions. Boykin (1979) outlines them:

1. Secondary market operations. Mortgage purchases by the corporation were to provide supplementary assistance to the housing market by increasing mortgage lenders' liquidity.

2. Special assistance function. Special programs, created by Congress or the President, were placed under the auspices of FNMA and funded by the U.S. Treasury.

3. Management and liquidating functions. All mortgages purchased before 1954 were to be managed by the government and eventually retired by FNMA.

Fannie Mae was viewed by Congress as primarily a reserve facility and was not allowed to make purchase commitments.[20] It was, however, allowed to raise its own funds under the protection of the Treasury and was designed to be self-supporting.

FNMA's activity increased dramatically after 1954. In 1957, during a period of tight credit, it purchased over 11 percent of all new single family mortgages originated that year. As credit conditions eased in 1958, FNMA sold much of its portfolio. Nevertheless by 1960, Fannie Mae held $2.9 billion in mortgages. By 1967 its portfolio grew to $5.5 billion.[21] Its impact in the mortgage market was far greater than that envisioned by Congress in 1954.[22]

1968 Housing and Urban Development Act   The movement of Fannie Mae from a public agency to a privately owned corporation began in 1954, was completed in 1968 as a result of Title VIII of the Housing and Urban Development Act (82 Stat. 536). Fannie Mae was chartered as a private, though government sponsored, corporation. It retained all assets, liabilities and functions that it had accumulated under Section 304 (secondary market operations) of the 1954 Act. A new agency—the Government National Mortgage Association (GNMA)—was created within HUD to assume responsibility for the other two functions originally assigned to Fannie Mae in 1954.

The new, private, Fannie Mae was set up with a 15 member board of directors. Of that number, five are appointed by the President (via the Secretary of HUD) and ten are elected by FNMA's private stockholders. Despite its status as a private corporation, the 1968 Act gave HUD some general regulatory authority over FNMA. Fannie Mae's structure, responsibilities and status have remained essentially the same since 1968.

Operations

Sources of Funds FNMA has several sources of funds available. Its principal source of funds is the sale of securities (debentures and discount notes). Debentures (sold in minimum lots of $10,000) have maturities which range from three to 25 years while its discount notes (sold in minimum lots of $50,000) have maturities which range from 30 to 270 days. Boykin (1979) argues that FNMA has attempted to achieve as long an average debt maturity as possible in order to avoid the expensive practice of frequently rolling over short term debt and better match the average maturity of its liabilities with the average maturity of its mortgage portfolio. Even though Fannie Mae is a private corporation, its securities still carry the status of federal agency securities, the characteristics of which were discussed earlier.

Since 1975, Fannie Mae has raised more than $100 billion in the money and capital markets, with $29.2 billion raised in 1980 alone. As of December 31, 1982 FNMA had in excess of $70 billion in outstanding debt, an increase of over 130 percent since 1975. Proceeds from the sale of debentures and notes has typically represented about 80% of total funds raised by FNMA each year.[23]

In addition to borrowings, Fannie Mae has several other sources of funds, FNMA has access to a $600 million line of credit with several banks, which it rarely uses. It may obtain long term funds by issuing FHA mortgage backed bonds which are guaranteed by GNMA, and are thus obligations of the U.S. Government. FNMA may also sell additional stock (which is traded on the NYSE); under its Charter, Fannie Mae has the power to require those who sell mortgages to the corporation to purchase its stock. Currently, there is no stock subscription requirement. Finally, FNMA receives funds from the commitment fees it charges, income from mortgages and other investments, and from the sale of mortgages to other investors.

As might be expected, FNMA's major uses of funds are purchasing mortgages and servicing debt. Table 6 presents summaries of FNMA's common size financial statements for 1979 and 1980.

Purchase Programs Fannie Mae's largest and most significant function is its secondary market operations. Its various purchase programs are the center of FNMA's secondary market operations.

Table 6. FNMA Common Size
Financial Statements
(1979 and 1980)

Balance Sheet

Assets	1980	1979
Cash and Marketable Securities	.9%	1.7%
Net Mortgage Portfolio	95.3	96.8
Other Assets	3.8	1.5

Liabilities & Capital		
Bonds, Notes and Debentures		
due within one year	27.1	25.9
due after one year	67.3	68.5
Other Liabilities	3.1	2.7
Stockholder's Equity	2.5	2.9

Income Statement

Income		
Interest & Discounts	98.7%	98.6%
Commitment Fees	1.2	1.2
Other Income	.1	.2

Expenses		
Net Interest	(94.5)	(87.1)
Other Expenses	(5.0)	(5.8)

Income Before Taxes	.5	7.1

Federal Income Taxes	(.3)	(3.8)

Income After Taxes	.2	3.3

Sources and Uses of Funds

Sources		
Operations	.5%	1.0%
Bonds, Debentures & Notes	86.1	78.7
Mortgage Principal Repayments	10.5	17.6
Other Sources	2.9	2.7

Uses		
Debt Repayments	43.3%	31.3%
Mortgage Purchases	50.1	68.0
Dividends	.4	.5
Increase in Cash and Short Term Investments	5.1	—
Other Uses	1.1	.2

Source: *FNMA Annual Report*, 1980, pp. 18–20.

Originally, FNMA was limited to purchasing FHA and VA mortgages. Since 1970, however, Fannie Mae may also purchase some types of conventional mortgages. Currently its home mortgage portfolio consists of 54.5 percent FHA-VA mortgages and 44.5 percent conventional mortgages.[24]

A seller of mortgages to Fannie Mae must have a net worth of at least $100,000 and usually continues to service mortgages for Fannie Mae. The normal servicing fee is ⅜ of one percent of the mortgage balance. FNMA will purchase mortgages with maturities of between 10 and 30 years. The maximum loan-to-value ratio is currently 95 percent.

At first, Fannie Mae purchased all mortgages over the counter; that is FNMA posted the prices it would pay for immediate delivery of mortgages on residential property. Boykin (1979) argues that this system was not efficient since it failed to "give lenders and builders sufficient assurance that funds would be available when needed" (p. 208).

To improve the efficiency of its purchase activity, FNMA instituted, in 1968, free market commitment auctions for conventional mortgages and FHA-VA mortgages. The prospective sellers made competitive bids for purchase commitments by specifying a dollar amount of loans and the yield these loans will produce to Fannie Mae. FNMA also accepted non-competitive bids; the prospective seller specified the dollar amount and agreed to accept the average yield on accepted competitive bids. In 1980, FNMA accepted 46.5 percent of FHA-VA mortgage commitments offered and 48.1 percent of conventional mortgage commitments offered.[25] Up until 1981, once a bid was accepted, the seller paid FNMA a fee of ½ of one percent of the commitment amount. The mortgage package, at the seller's option, could be sold to Fannie Mae at any time during the four month commitment period. From 1968 to 1981, Fannie May purchased the vast majority of mortgages using commitments.

Thus, the successful bidder obtained what was effectively a put option. Even if interest rates soared during the four month commitment period, FNMA still had to purchase the mortgage package at the agreed upon yield. By issuing forward purchase commitments, Fannie Mae assumed a great deal of interest rate risk, especially in a period of highly unstable interest rates.

In late 1981, FNMA instituted several new mortgage purchase programs in an attempt to rely less on forward purchase commitments and thus assume less interest rate risk. FNMA now posts the prices it will pay for mortgages delivered at any time during a one or two month period. Unlike purchase commitments, delivery on the part of the seller is mandatory. FNMA also raised the fee on forward purchase commitments to 2 percent of the commitment amount. The combination of these changes lead to a sharp reduction in purchase commitment auction activity during 1982. FNMA

Table 7.   FNMA Activity Since 1960
(Millions of Dollars)

Year	Commitments	Purchases	Sales	Year-End Portfolio	Net Savings Inflows*
1960	**	980	42	2,903	7,559
1965	**	757	46	2,520	8,513
1966	1,920	2,081	***	4,396	3,615
1967	1,736	1,400	12	5,522	10,649
1968	2,697	1,944	–0–	7,167	7,478
1969	6,630	4,121	–0–	10,950	4,079
1970	8,047	5,078	–0–	15,502	11,018
1971	9,828	3,574	336	17,791	27,974
1972	8,797	3,699	211	19,791	32,663
1973	8,914	6,127	71	24,175	20,237
1974	10,765	6,953	4	29,578	16,068
1975	6,106	4,263	2	31,824	42,806
1976	6,247	3,606	86	32,904	50,585
1977	9,729	4,780	67	34,370	51,016
1978	18,959	12,303	5	43,311	44,864
1979	10,179	10,805	–0–	51,097	39,304
1980	8,044	8,100	–0–	55,104	41,417
1981	9,331	6,112	2	58,675	13,425

*   - inflows to SLAs only
**   - data not available
*** - less than $500,000
Source: *Federal Reserve Bulletin*, various issues.

announced in early 1983 that the forward purchase commitment auctions were being suspended.

Table 7 summarizes FNMA purchase and sale activity from 1960 to 1981. Since 1960, Fannie Mae has purchased between $757 million and $12.3 billion worth of mortgages in a single year. Its total portfolio has grown from less than $3 billion in 1960 to over $58 billion in 1980 (an increase of 1800 percent). Table 7 also illustrates the relationship between purchases and purchase commitment volume. Only in 1966, 1979 and 1980 did yearly purchases exceed commitments issued. These data indicate not all purchase commitments are "taken down."

Three Current Issues

Portfolio Size   FNMA's total mortgage portfolio has risen every year since 1965 (see table 7). Only in 1971 and 1972 did Fannie Mae sales top $100 million; in both these years FNMA purchases were over $3.5 billion. Table 5 illustrates the relationship between savings flows and FNMA purchases.

Given the countercyclical nature of FNMA purchases, it is not surprising that Fannie Mae purchased large amounts of mortgages in years of relatively low savings inflows (1970, and 1974). However, in 1977, when savings inflows were a record $51 billion, Fannie Mae still purchased over $4.7 billion in mortgages. In 1978, when savings flows topped $44 billion, FNMA purchased a record $12.5 billion in mortgages.

This behavior raises questions about the function of FNMA as a true secondary market operation; some argue that FNMA has become a lender with a permanent loan portfolio rather than a market making operation. The U.S. Department of Housing and Urban Development, for one, suggests that FNMA's policies on sales and purchases are inconsistent with its charter:

> FNMA maintains a mortgage portfolio larger than necessary to accomplish the public purposes of the Charter Act. Moreover, it has failed to balance purchases with sales when this was feasible. (43 Fed. Reg. 36204).

Fannie Mae responds that a study conducted by the Congressional Research Service of the Library of Congress concluded that FNMA could not have undertaken significant mortgage sales in recent years without major costs to home buyers and the home finance industry.[26]

Financial Performance   Given the fact that FNMA uses primarily borrowed funds to purchase mortgages, high interest rates during the last two years have taken their toll on FNMA's financial condition. Fannie Mae's average cost of debt (both new and existing) rose from less than eight percent in 1978 to over ten percent in 1980. At the same time, the average yield on its primarily fixed rate mortgage portfolio rose from 8.25 percent in 1978 to 9.25 percent in 1980.[27] Unsettled conditions in the financial markets have also forced Fannie Mae to borrow more short term funds relative to long term funds. The result has been a decline in the average maturity of its debt from 53 months in 1977 to 35 months in 1980.[28]

FNMA lost over $41 million on its mortgage portfolio in 1980, compared to a $241 million profit in 1979. Income from other sources, such as commitment fees, kept Fannie Mae in the black overall in 1980; it earned $.23 a share.[29] The first half of 1981 proved to be even worse, FNMA lost $40.1 million.[30]

As a result, Fannie Mae announced in June 1981 that it would start purchasing eight types of mortgages with variable rates. Considering the size of its fixed rate portfolio, this change may have little impact on FNMA's financial performance as long as interest rates remain high.

Relationship with HUD   The 1968 Charter Act, together with its legislative history, indicates that Congress intended that some governmental control over FNMA remain despite the transfer of ownership to private hands. Congress wanted to make sure that adequate safeguards existed to insure that the public purposes of the 1968 Act were carried out. For example, the Secretary of HUD, in addition to appointing several members of FNMA's Board, must approve several specific actions. FNMA must also, under the 1968 Act, secure prior approval of the Treasury in conjunction with several aspects of its financing.

Since HUD was given most of the regulatory responsibility over FNMA, HUD issued a set of proposed and final regulations in 1978 (43 Fed. Reg. 36200). The preamble to the final regulations (pp. 36200–36205)—a preamble lacks legal force—was sharply critical of Fannie Mae's conduct of its secondary market operations. Both the proposed regulations and preamble to final regulations created a great deal of controversy.[31]

HUD asserted, in the preamble, that FNMA was required by its Charter to perform certain public services. There were in return for the benefits, conferred on FNMA by Congress (such as borrowing funds under the more favorable terms accorded federal agency securities)—benefits not available to most private corporations. The preamble goes on to argue that Congress intended HUD to have broad regulatory authority over FNMA in order to see that all aspects of the 1968 Act were carried out.

HUD charged that FNMA has failed to accomplish many of its public policy objectives. Specifically, HUD argued that FNMA has failed to: one, provide enough support to housing for low and moderate income families and two, provide sufficient capital to inner city areas, where it is often difficult to obtain mortgage credit.

FNMA took exception to much of the preamble. First, Fannie Mae argued that HUD exaggerated the benefits conferred on FNMA by Congress in 1968. Second, FNMA argued that HUD misinterpreted FNMA's role as a result of the 1968 Act. Specifically the fact that many of the policy objectives HUD said were FNMA's responsibility, were in actuality assigned to GNMA. Third, Fannie Mae charged that HUD overstated its role as FNMA regulator; HUD does not have plenary power over FNMA, its regulatory authority is limited to specifically enumerated powers. Finally, Fannie Mae took exception to HUD's assertion that it was not doing enough to meet the housing needs of low and moderate income families, or helping inner-city areas obtain adequate mortgage credit.

HUD proposed a set of regulations that would have severely restricted FNMA's operations. Among other things, HUD would have assumed much more control over FNMA's finances. In addition, mandatory credit allocations would have required that 30 percent of FNMA's mortgage purchases be allocated to each of the following three categories of mortgages: inner-city housing, existing housing and housing for low and moderate income families.

The proposed regulations were criticized by FNMA, much of the home finance industry and members of Congress. HUD dropped the mandatory quotas and softened many other regulations. In place of quotas, HUD set forth a procedure by which FNMA and HUD would jointly set "general" goals designed to meet public policy objectives. FNMA summarized its reaction to HUD's final regulations as follows:

> ... the tone of the preamble is not reflected in the final regulations which clearly envision a working partnership between HUD and FNMA. The changes in HUD's regulations accommodate FNMA's role as an independent, shareholder controlled private corporation.
>
> The needs of the American people for decent, safe and affordable housing will be met by a cooperative partnership between the public and private sectors. The "preamble" aside, HUD's final regulations provide an opportunity for such a partnership between HUD and FNMA. (1979 General Counsel's Report, p. 221).

Government National Mortgage Association

History

The Government National Mortgage Association (or Ginnie Mae) was created in 1968. Unlike FNMA, Ginnie Mae is a government corporation, without capital stock or a board of directors. It is wholly a part of HUD.

The 1968 HUD Act assigned two functions to GNMA previously the responsibility of FNMA: the special assistance function and the management and liquidation function. Congress felt that neither function could justifiably be carried out by the private sector. Ginnie Mae was also authorized to begin a mortgage backed security program by the 1968 Act.

GNMA receives no direct congressional appropriations. It obtains funds from borrowings from the Treasury, receipts from operations and proceeds from mortgage sales. Any security issued by Ginnie Mae carries the full faith and credit of the U.S. Government, and thus has no default risk.

Functions and Programs

Special Assistance Function (SAF) Ginnie Mae is assigned the role of purchasing mortgages that would not be marketable without assistance. Like FNMA, GNMA issues purchase commitments to primary lenders. They can be for up to three years for certain multi-family loans and up to one year for single family loans. Commitment fees vary depending on the type of loan.

Essentially the special assistance function may be broken down into two responsibilities. The first is to purchase FHA-VA loans which provide housing to low and moderate income families. The second is to purchase all types of loans in order to stimulate housing sales and construction during periods of tight credit. The first responsibility was assigned to Ginnie Mae in 1968 while the second was assigned to GNMA as a result of the 1974 Emergency Home Purchase Assistance Act (88 Stat. 1364) and the 1975 Emergency Housing Act (89 Stat. 249).

Table 8 indicates that SAF purchases by GNMA have followed the performance of the economy. Between 1970 and 1973, the SAF portfolio was relatively stable. However, as credit conditions tightened in 1974 and 1975, GNMA purchases increased sharply. An easing of credit, starting in 1976, allowed GNMA to reduce the size of its SAF portfolio; it declined from over $6.8 billion in 1975 to $2.5 billion in 1978. Economic conditions recently have necessitated increased GNMA purchases, although its SAF portfolio at the end of 1981 was still well below the 1975 level.

Management and Liquidation Function (MLF) in 1954 FNMA was charged with the responsibility of managing and liquidating mortgages the federal government had acquired between 1938 and 1954. GNMA was assigned this responsibility in 1968. In addition, GNMA also took over the

Table 8.   Summary of GNMA Operations (Millions of Dollars)

		Mortgage Portfolio (year end)		GNMA Pass-Throughs	
Year	Total	Special Assistance	Management & Liquidation	Issued (during year)	Outstanding (year-end)
1969	4,865	2,937	1,928	—	—
1970	5,222	3,401	1,821	452	452
1971	5,321	3,648	1,673	2,702	2,850
1972	5,111	3,824	1,287	2,662	5,504
1973	4,045	3,576	489	3,249	7,890
1974	4,849	4,440	409	4,784	11,769
1975	7,242	6,884	358	7,366	18,257
1976	4,407	4,102	305	13,765	30,572
1977	3,249	2,989	260	16,230	44,896
1978	2,741	2,521	220	15,359	54,347
1979	3,377	3,181	196	22,020	76,401
1980	4,383	4,215	168	22,996	93,874
1981	3,839	3,698	141	14,253	105,790

Source *GNMA Annual Report,* 1971–1981.

management of mortgages FNMA had acquired from the Housing and Home Finance Administration between 1959 and 1967.

As shown by table 8, Ginnie Mae has reduced the size of this portfolio steadily since 1968. Originally assigned over $1.9 billion in mortgages to manage and liquidate in 1968, Ginnie Mae has reduced its MLF portfolio to approximately $141 million.

Mortgage-Backed Security Program Perhaps the most significant impact of Ginnie Mae on the mortgage market has been its mortgage backed security program. Under Section 306 (g) of the 1968 HUD Act, GNMA was authorized to guarantee timely payment of principal and interest on long term securities backed by a self-liquidating pool of mortgages. The pool consists of loans insured or guaranteed by FHA, VA or the Farmers' Home Administration. Unlike other federal secondary mortgage market programs, the FSCA—Ginnie Mae in this case—never actually purchases any portion of the mortgage pool.

Two types of securities are eligible for guarantee. The first is a "bond-type" security which pays its holder interest semi-annually and principal at stated times. GNMA guarantees payment of principal and interest on bonds actually issued by FNMA or the Mortgage Corporation. The bonds are backed by a pool of mortgages. This type of security is rarely issued, the last time being in 1979. At the end of 1980, less than $1 billion in "bond-type" GNMA securities were outstanding.[32]

The other type is called a pass-through security. The issuer collects mortgagors' monthly principal and interest payments and passes them on to the security holder. Pass-throughs are issued by approximately 500 mortgage companies and thrift institutions. The issuer originates the mortgages (all must have the same maturity and interest rate), packages them into an aggregate amount (minimum of $1 million) and converts the pool of loans into a GNMA security.[33]

This program has proven to be extemely popular. Boileau (1977) writes: "many investors have been attracted to this security because it combines the best features of mortgages and government bonds: safety, yield marketability and cash flow" (p. 20). In fact the largest single holder of GNMA pass-throughs is savings and loan associations.[34]

Since 1971 the amount of GNMA pass-throughs issued in any one year has ranged from a low of $2.7 billion in 1972 to a high of over $22.9 billion in 1980. As of December 31, 1981, over 105 billion in Ginnie Mae pass-throughs were outstanding. Pass-through activity is illustrated in table 6.

Tandem Plans Tandem plans are special relationships between Ginnie Mae and other mortgage investors, although most tandem activities have been with Fannie Mae. Tandem programs were first established in 1970 and were designed to stimulate construction and rehabilitation of housing, especially for low and moderate income families.

Under one tandem plan, Ginnie Mae issues a commitment to a primary lender to purchase a loan at a specified price. After GNMA acquires the loan, it sells the loan to FNMA at prevailing market prices. GNMA absorbs any discount from the price paid the original seller. In another type of tandem plan, first begun in 1974, FNMA or the Mortgage Corporation issues a commitment to purchase below market rate mortgages provided the lower rate is passed on to borrowers. When the loans are delivered to FNMA or the Corporation, GNMA absorbs the discount.

Federal Home Loan Mortgage Corporation

History

The Federal Home Loan Mortgage Corporation (known since 1976 as the Mortgage Corporation) was established in 1970 by Title III of the Emergency Home Finance Act (84 Stat. 450). It was established to increase the supply of mortgage funds, improve the attractiveness of mortgage instruments, and give mortgage investors greater flexibility.

The 1970 Act placed FHLMC under the direction and supervision of the Federal Home Loan Bank Board. By statute, and Bank Board regulation, the FHLB Board sets general policy dealing with FHLMC operations and financing. In addition, the FHLB Board chairman acts as the chairman of FHLMC's board of directors. By law, the Corporation may deal only with federally supervised lenders—usually depository institutions—and mortgage bankers approved by the Bank Board.[35]

The Corporation was initially funded by $100 million in nonvoting stock issued only to FHLB Banks. Thus indirectly, the Mortgage Corporation is owned by FHLB member institutions. In addition to the stock, FHLMC obtains funds from: sales of GNMA backed securities, borrowings from FHLB Banks, operating income and mortgage sales.

Secondary Market Operations

Purchase Programs Like Fannie Mae, the Mortgage Corporation is authorized to purchase FHA, VA and conventional mortgages over-the-counter or by issuing forward purchase commitments. The Corporation may purchase whole loans (i.e., 100 percent of the loan amount), or purchase between 50 and 85 percent interest in specific types of mortgages, these are called participation loan purchases.[36] FLHMC also acts as an agent for

Ginnie Mae in issuing commitments to purchase conventional single family mortgages at below market interest rates. Table 9 shows Mortgage Corporation purchase activity since 1970. Between 1970 and 1972, the Corporation purchased primarily FHA and VA mortgages. Beginning in 1973, however, FHLMC has started to purchase mostly conventional loans. Since 1976, the Corporation has purchased less than $100 million in FHA and VA mortgages, while purchasing over $17 billion in conventional mortgages.

Table 9 also illustrates the counter-cyclical relationship between purchases and credit conditions. Unlike Fannie Mae, the Corporation has sharply reduced purchase activity in years of relatively easy credit. FHLMC's total mortgage portfolio actually declined between 1975 and 1978, from $4.9 billion in 1975 to approximately $3 billion in 1978.

Sales Program   The 1970 Act, along with its legislative history, suggests that Congress intended the Corporation to become a true secondary market agency, not merely an accumulator of mortgages.[37] As a result, the Corporation's sales programs have become as important as its purchase programs. Mortgage sales provide most of the Corporation's funds.

The Corporation does not actually sell individual mortgages to other investors, rather it sells certificates which represent part ownership in a large pool of loans distributed throughout the United States. There are two types of FHLMC certificates.

The first is called a guaranteed mortgage certification (GMC). The GMC was designed for institutional investors who traditionally did not invest in mortgages. It pays investors interest semi-annually as well as a minimum annual principal payment. The principal payment can be, and often is, greater than the specified minimum. GMCs, thus, offer certain investors two important advantages over pass-through mortgage instruments: greater certainty of payment and a more bond-like instrument. GMCs have been purchased by trusts, commercial banks, pension funds and insurance companies.

The other type of mortgage certificate issued by the Corporation is called a participation certificate (PC). PCs represent, for regulatory and tax purposes, actual ownership of residential mortgages. They are, therefore, attractive to savings and loan associations, which must keep a certain percentage of their assets in mortgages.[38] Similar to GNMA pass-throughs, PCs pay investors interest and principal monthly and are unconditionally guaranteed by the Corporation. PCs differ from GNMA pass-throughs in a number of ways. For example, PCs represent interests in conventional loans while GNMAs represent interests in FHA, VA or Farmers' Home loans.

Table 9 illustrates GMC and PC sales since 1970. PCs have been far more popular, over $21 billion have been sold since the program started in

Table 9. The Mortgage Corporation—Summary of Operations (Millions of Dollars)

| Year | Holdings (end of year) | | | Transactions (during year) | | | | Purchase Commitments Made |
| | Total | FHA-VA | Conventional | Purchases | | Sales | | |
				FHA-VA	Conventional	PCs	GMCs	
1970	325	325	—	325	—	—	—	518
1971	968	821	147	564	214	65	—	801
1972	1,788	1,502	286	833	464	317	—	1,606
1973	2,604	1,800	804	335	999	409	—	1,629
1974	4,586	1,961	2,625	261	1,929	53	—	4,553
1975	4,987	1,881	3,106	119	1,594	951	500	982
1976	4,269	1,675	2,594	20	1,107	1,362	400	1,478
1977	3,267	1,450	1,817	20	4,140	4,033	600	5,501
1978	3,091	1,299	1,792	40	6,486	5,726	700	7,510
1979	4,052	1,159	2,893	—	5,721	3,794	750	5,542
1980	5,056	1,090	3,966	1	3,722	2,526	—	3,859
1981	5,237	1,047	4,190	—	3,789	3,532	—	6,974

Source: FHLB Journal, June 1982.

1971. By contrast, less than $3 billion in GMCs have been issued. Not surprisingly, sales of both types of certificates have been heaviest during years of relatively high savings inflows.

Summary

Chapter 2 outlines the history and functions of the four federal mortgage agencies. The Federal Home Loan Bank Board, the Federal National Mortgage Association, the Government National Mortgage Association and the Federal Home Loan Mortgage Corporation are responsible for implementing policies designed to stabilize and increase the availability of mortgage credit.

In order to thoroughly evaluate the effectiveness of federal mortgage policy at meeting its primary policy objectives, and in order to determine what impacts these policies may have on other market participants, it is necessary to understand the historical background of each of the federal mortgage agencies. In addition, examining their current operations illustrates just how extensive and important their activities are to the housing and mortgage markets.

3

Summary of Relevant Literatures

Introduction

The purpose of chapter 3 is to summarize two literatures which are highly relevant to this study. The first literature contains studies which have examined the relationship between the availability of mortgage credit and housing construction activity. The second literature contains studies which have attempted to ascertain the effectiveness of federal mortgage agency activities—FHLB advances and FSCA secondary market operations—at increasing and stabilizing the availability of mortgage credit. Since federal policy is based on the notion that increasing (stabilizing) the availability of mortgage credit will increase (stabilize) housing construction activity, an understanding of both literatures is necessary.

This review does not seek to be all inclusive, rather it attempts to summarize findings and trends in the two literatures. Several reviews currently exist which are more comprehensive.[1]

Credit Availability Hypothesis

The first literature to be reviewed in this chapter deals with the relationship between the cost and availability of mortgage credit and the post World War II cycles in housing construction activity. The credit availability hypothesis states that credit considerations, whether they work through mortgage demand or supply, were primarily responsible for post-war housing construction cycles.

Guttentag (1961) and Alberts (1962) were among the first to address the credit availability hypothesis. Both studies involved nonquantitative examinations of historical data on housing starts, mortgage lending, deposit flows to financial institutions and so forth. Both argued that mortgages are considered by financial institutions to be residual investments. Guttentag specifically identified the role of corporate financing in determining mortgage credit availability.

> . . . the volume of mortgage credit is a sort of residual in that home buyers can obtain only that volume of credit which remains after the more volatile and persistent demands of corporations have been satisfied. (p. 292).

One of his primary pieces of evidence is a chart showing net changes in outstanding mortgage debt and outstanding corporate debt from 1949 to 1960. The two series are virtually mirror images of each other.

As the flow of funds to financial institutions slows, less capital exists for residual investments and consequently the flow of funds into the mortgage market falls. As this happened historically, Guttentag and Alberts argued that higher mortgage rates and credit rationing resulted.

Guttentag argued that, in the short run, mortgage demand is dominated by credit considerations. Since other demand factors—income, population, and so forth—do not change significantly in the short run, cycles in the cost and availability of credit lead to short cycles in mortgage demand, and thus housing construction activity.

Although Alberts reached much the same overall conclusion about the effect of credit availability on residential construction activity, his explanation differed somewhat from Guttentag's. Alberts argued that the demand for mortgage credit changes only slightly during the business cycle in relationship to the supply of mortgage funds. He argued that shifts in mortgage supply during the business cycle are due to changes in relative yields between mortgages and bonds. Therefore, Alberts suggested that changes in the supply of credit have been primarily responsible for changes in housing construction activity.

Econometric Evidence

Soon after the argument was initially advanced that credit considerations were the keys to explaining housing construction cycles, econometric studies began to appear which addressed the same issue. These studies addressed the credit availability hypothesis specifically or as part of larger macroeconomic models.

Two of the most significant of the early econometric studies were conducted by S. J. Maisel. Maisel (1963, 1965) concluded that the cyclical behavior of construction activity was analogous to inventory cycles. He suggested that an underlying demand existed which formed a relatively stable equilibrium. Maisel argued that the construction process created shifts in inventories and vacancies which lead to shifts in housing starts around the basic demand equilibrium. Housing starts are influenced by credit considerations through inventories and vacancies. Demand, on the other hand, appeared to be relatively unaffected by credit considerations, Maisel argued.

In a later study, Maisel (1968) found that the availability of mortgage credit was an important determinant of housing construction activity in the short run. Maisel argued that the mortgage rate was not necessarily a sufficient indicator of conditions in the mortgage market, since consumers might not be able to obtain a mortgage at the current rate. Thus, credit rationing also played an important role in determining short term shifts in housing starts. Maisel estimated that a one percent increase in the mortgage rate would lead to a 143,000 unit decrease in housing starts, while a $1 billion decrease in deposit flows to savings and loans would result in a 33,000 unit decrease in housing starts.

Two studies by D. S. Huang (1966, 1969) also tested the credit availability hypothesis. In contrast to Maisel (1963, 1965), who found little relationship between credit and mortgage demand, Huang (1966) determined that changes in the loan amortization period had a positive relationship with mortgage demand. His 1969 study developed a supply-demand structural model of both the mortgage and housing markets. In general, Huang concluded that credit terms (amortization period, maximum loan-to-value ratio and mortgage rate) as well as the overall availability of credit were important determinants of mortgage lending and housing construction activity.

Several other econometric studies were conducted from the mid-sixties to 1970.[2] To one degree or another, these studies provide additional evidence in support of the credit availability hypothesis. For example, Swan (1970) found a strong, positive relationship between housing starts and savings flows to mutual savings banks and savings and loans.

Prior to 1970, most econometric studies tested the credit availability hypothesis by adding measures of credit availability to essentially single equation explanations of housing construction activity. More recent work has attempted to estimate both supply and demand functions for housing.

Fair (1971) developd a monthly model of housing starts which included both supply and demand functions. Fair also explicitly allowed for market disequilibrium (i.e., the mortgage rate failed to clear the market). Overall, his results tend to support the credit availability hypothesis. Measures of credit availability were included in both the demand and supply equations. Resulting coefficients were correctly signed and statistically significant.

Critique of the Credit Availability Hypothesis

In spite of the evidence in support of the credit availabiltiy hypothesis, some have argued that the link between the cost and availability of credit, housing demand and housing construction activity may be, at best, weak and indirect. Perhaps the most vocal dissenter is Allan Meltzer. Meltzer (1974) argued that the conclusion reached by most studies that both cost and availability of credit were important in determining short-run fluctuations in housing activity was simply wrong.

Meltzer presented two types of evidence in support of his conclusion. The first consisted of long-term data on the composition of household assets and liabilities. He examined trends in three ratios: housing to total assets, mortgage debt to housing; and mortgage debt to total liabilities. After examining these data, Meltzer concluded:

> There is evidence that the considerable increase in the relative use of mortgages has had any effect on the distribution between housing and other assets. There is, therefore, no evidence that changes in the composition of 'credit' have any long-term effect on the composition of assets (pp. 765–66).

Meltzer's second type of evidence consisted of results of several econometric studies which, he claimed, provided evidence in support of this position. Dhrymes and Taubman (1969), in a study of the savings and loan industry, examined the impact of mortgage terms and conditions on mortgage demand. They concluded:

> In all equations where maturity was added, it had an incorrect negative sign. We concluded, therefore, that the mortgage rage is the only term of the mortgage important in determining the demand for mortgages (p. 115).

Meltzer argued that this result is significant, especially in light of a conclusion reached by Jaffee (1972). Jaffee found that changes in mortgage flows appeared to have little impact on mortgage rates. Consequently, doubt is cast on the effectiveness of increasing the availability of mortgage credit to stimulate the demand for mortgages and housing starts.

Meltzer's major empirical work—Arcelus and Meltzer (1973)—was also cited as evidence. Their model consisted of three equations measuring the demand for housing services, the supply of new homes and the demand for new homes. Arcelus and Meltzer concluded that no evidence existed that either the supply of or demand for housing increased with increases in the stock or flow of mortgage credit.

Meltzer's conclusions have been strongly criticized. In a detailed review of Arcelus and Meltzer, Swan (1973) wrote:

> ... their attempt is fatally marred by serious errors in the specification of their model, the absence of any acceptable econometric evidence, and serious errors in their simulation experiments. In view of these shortcomings one must conlude that A-M have offered no convincing evidence to discredit the conventional wisdom or to support their own view of housing markets (p. 971).

In a review of the credit availability literature, Kearl, Rosen and Swan (1975) also criticized Meltzer's conclusions. It is unlikely, they suggested, that few researchers who found evidence of credit rationing would have argued that credit availability has determined the long-run equilibrium housing stock. Instead these researchers were more concerned with short-run cyclical fluctuations and felt that the availability of credit was an important—perhaps most important—short-run constraint. Therefore, the distinction between short-run adjustment behavior and long-run equilibrium must be made. They argued that Meltzer failed to make this distinction in arriving at his conclusions. For example, Arcelus and Meltzer used long time series of annual data while most other econometric studies used post-war quarterly or monthly data.

Illiquidity Hypothesis

In a recent study, Kearl and Mishkin (1977) suggested another possible hypothesis to explain short cyles in housing starts. They argued that the illiquid nature of housing could explain much of the variation in housing construction activity since the end of WW II. Their argument may be summarized as follows:

> The liquidity hypothesis indicates that the illiquid nature of the housing asset forces the consumer to take account of his debt and gross financial asset position as well as the riskiness of his income stream in determining the desired level of his housing stock (p. 1573).

Thus households will alter their demand for housing in response to changes in expected income, the variance of expected income and current debt holdings.

The illiquidity hypothesis was tested by estimating single equation models of single and multi-family housing starts using quarterly data. Initially, the equations were estimated with illiquidity variables and without credit availability variables. Then the equations were re-estimated including credit availability measures. The models proved to be adequate without the credit variables, and the coefficients of the credit variables, once included, were not statistically significant.[3] This lead Kearl and Mishkin to conclude:

> Tests of credit rationing effects on housing demand pursued here do not resolve the controversy over whether these effects do indeed exist. (The data) indicate that the credit availability doctrine is by no means needed to explain the postwar residential housing cycle (pp. 1582–83).

The literature pertaining to the credit availability hypothesis is extensive and has only been summarized here. Essentially most of the available evidence (both historical and econometric) suggests that the cost and availability of mortgage credit are important short-run determinants of mortgage lending and housing construction activity. This is true whether credit considerations work primarily through mortgage demand (as Huang, and others, argued) or through inventories and vacancies (as Maisel argued).

Despite some deficiencies, Meltzer's conclusions cannot be totally ignored. Neither can the illiquidity hypothesis advanced by Kearl and Mishkin be dismissed. Nonetheless, the weight of evidence supports, to one extent or another, the credit availability hypothesis. Thus, there appears to be an economic rationale for federal programs designed to increase and stabilize the availability of mortgage credit.

Effectiveness of Federal Mortgage Policy

The second literature to be reviewed in this chapter consists of studies which have directly, or indirectly, examined the effectiveness of federal programs designed to increase and stabilize the availability of mortgage credit. These studies may be divided into two general groups: studies which treat FHLB advances and FSCA purchases as exogenous variables and studies which treat agency actions as endogenous variables.

Exogenous Variable Studies

Many of the studies which treat agency actions as exogenous variables tested their effectiveness by including measures of FHLB advances and FSCA purchases in larger econometric studies of the housing and mortgage markets; some of these studies were discussed in the previous section. Principal results were somewhat mixed.

Huang (1969) included FHLB advances and FNMA purchases in equations explaining housing starts and equations explaining mortgage lending. Huang found that both FHLB and FNMA actions had significant, positive impacts on the level of housing starts and the supply of some mortgage loans. Huang wrote:

> With respect to the activities of FNMA and FHLB, the evidence here is that the FNMA net purchases and the FHLB's net advances respectively are strongly associated with the extension of VA and conventional loans (p. 1231).

In contrast to Huang, Schwartz (1970) argued that FNMA activity appeared to be more countercyclical than FHLB activity, in that FNMA purchases were better able to counteract the cyclical behavior of housing starts. Swan (1970), Brady (1970) and Fair (1972), on the other hand, presented evidence that FHLB advances had a positive impact on the housing and mortgage markets while FNMA purchases had no net effect.

Jaffee (1972) examined both the short and long run effectiveness of FHLB and FNMA actions. His results were quite pessimistic in the case of FNMA, and only somewhat more optimistic in FHLB's case. FNMA purchases, Jaffee determined, had only a small short run impact on the availability of mortgage credit and no long term impact. He wrote; ". . . in the long run it appeared the net effect of FNMA policy would be about zero" (p. 178). In the case of FHLB advances, Jaffee suggested that "variations in the FHLB borrowing rate have significant effects in the model in both the long run and short run" (p. 178). However, the use of the FHLB advance rate depends upon how well it can be made to vary independently from market interest rates. Aside from the advance rate, Jaffee argued that the quantity of advances had a significant short run impact, but no real long term impact on the supply of mortgage credit.

Endogenous Variable Studies

One of the first studies which treated FHLB and FNMA actions as endogenous variables was Silber (1973). He argued that previous studies which drew conclusions about the overall effectiveness of FHLB and FNMA actions were seriously flawed from two major reasons. First, these studies failed to take into account the endogenous nature of agency actions, which may explain some conclusions of these studies.

> Our results suggest that the inability to find a positive impact of FNMA activity results from the failure to take into account the endogenous nature of both FNMA and FHLB activity (p. 309).

Essentially, agencies respond directly or indirectly to mortgage market conditions. Therefore, Silber argued that their actions should be treated as dependent, not independent variables.[4] Silber's second criticism was with the inclusion of FHLB and FNMA variables in a single equation with housing starts as the dependent variable and mortgage flows as an additional independent variable. Since both agencies respond to the same phenomena, Silber argued that such an equation would likely suffer from multicollinearity problems.

Silber constructed and estimated equations which modeled FHLB and FNMA behavior. Silber's equations were based upon the notion that both agencies attempt to minimize the deviation of actual housing starts from the desired level of housing starts. Results provide some evidence that FHLB and FNMA actions were successful in meeting their countercyclical policy objectives.

A more detailed study of FHLB and FNMA activities was conducted by Kearl and Rosen (1974). While agreeing with Silber's argument concerning the endogenous nature of agency activity, Kearl and Rosen asserted that Silber made several faulty interpretations and attempted to test complicated structural relationships with simple models. To overcome this, Kearl and Rosen constructed a structural model which specified relationships between the agencies and both the housing and mortgage markets. Their model also allowed for interrelationships between the housing and mortgage markets. Kearl and Rosen present evidence that both FNMA and FHLB activities significantly increased the availability of mortgage credit; FNMA purchases were judged to be slightly more significant than FHLB advances. They wrote that "in contrast to previous studies we have found that both FHLB and FNMA have a significant positive impact on the supply of mortgages" (p. 25).

Both Kearl and Rosen (1974) and Silber (1973) may be viewed as being short-run studies. What this means is that their studies were structured to examine only the short term effectiveness of federal agency activity. Two simulation studies, Hendershott and Villani (1977) and Jaffee and Rosen (1978), attempted to examine both short and long run effectiveness. The studies simulated the impact, on the housing and mortgage markets, of various FSCA and FHLB actions.[5] Both studies provided evidence which strongly suggests that agency activity has a significant short term (i.e., less than one year) impact on the supply of mortgage credit, but have less than a significant impact on the long term supply of credit.

Jaffee and Rosen, for example, simulate the impact of an increase in FSCA purchase commitments of $18 billion during a period of tight credit. Four months later, outstanding mortgage loans at savings and loan associations have increased by $3.2 billion, seven months later the increase is $3.8 billion. However, after seven months, reactions by other market participants reduce the impact of the policy shock and 12 months after the shock, outstanding loans have increased by only $415 million.

Recent studies have examined the behavior of federal mortgage agencies, and tested their effectiveness, by taking a somewhat different approach. Rosen and Bloom (1980) and Kent (1981) developed microeconomic models of agency behavior; they examined specific agencies individually.

Rosen and Bloom examined the Federal Home Loan Mortgage Corporation (FHLMC) by developing a model of the FHLMC mortgage commitment mechanism. The model consisted of commitment demand and supply equations. Results provided evidence of the countercyclical effectiveness of the FHLMC commitment process.

> In conclusion, it appears that the FHLMC has designed a commitment mechanism which does respond in a countercyclical fashion to the credit demands of mortgage market participants (p. 970).

Kent (1981) specifically examined the effectiveness of three FHLB policies aimed at reducing fluctuations in the mortgage market (two special advance programs and changes in the minimum liquidity ratio). Kent developed and estimated a portfolio allocation model for savings and loan associations. His results raise serious questions about the effectiveness of special advance programs at increasing and stabilizing the availability of mortgage credit.

> In 1970 and again in 1974 special advance programs were established. In both periods most of the net increase in borrowings was not lent in the mortgage market; rather it was invested in other assets such as government bonds (p. 77).

In conclusion, while the literature dealing with the effectiveness of federal agency activity is not as voluminous as the credit availability literature, it is nonetheless extensive. If one general conclusion may be drawn from this literature it is that the weight of evidence seems to suggest that federal mortgage agencies are relatively effective at meeting their primary policy objectives—increasing and stablizing the availability of mortgage credit—in the short run and less than effective in meeting objectives in the long run.

Summary

This chapter has summarized two literatures important to this study. The first literature deals with the relationship between the cost and availability of mortgage credit and housing construction activity. This literature suggests both the cost and availability of credit are important determinants of the short cycle in housing construction activity. The second literature examines the effectiveness of federal mortgage agency activity at expanding the availability of credit. The most current studies appear to indicate that agency activities are effective in the short run, but relatively ineffective in the long run.

4

Theory and Methodology

Introduction

Chapter 4 introduces a theoretical model which illustrates key relationships among various markets and participants. From this model, two testable hypotheses about some of the effects of FHLB and FSCA activities on financial markets and institutions will be developed.

Theoretical Framework

The purpose of federal mortgage agency activity is to increase and stabilize the availability of mortgage credit. In theory, this will allow housing construction activity to obtain a larger, more stable share of GNP. In reality, however, accumulated theoretical and empirical evidence strongly suggests that agency activities have no significant impact on either the housing or mortgage markets over extended periods of time. This is due, perhaps, to reactions by private market participants to changes in relative interest rates induced by the activities of federal mortgage agencies.

A simple model, which illustrates key relationships among various markets and participants, will be introduced here. This model is a modified version of a model developed by Jaffee and Rosen (1978).[1] From this model, testable hypotheses concerning the effects of agency activities on the financial markets will be developed.

Omitting exogenous variables, the following relationships are theorized to exist:

$$\text{deposit flows} = D = f(R, \dots) \tag{1}$$

$$\text{mortgage supply} = M^s = f(D, Rm, R, A, \dots) \tag{2}$$

$$\text{mortgage demand} = M^d = f(H, Rm, \dots) \tag{3}$$

$$\text{mortgage loans made} = M = \min(M^s, M^d) \tag{4}$$

housing starts = H = f(M, Rm, . . .)   (5)

agency activity = A = f(H − H*, D, . . .)   (6)

capital market interest rate = R = f(A, . . .)   (7)

D, M^s, M^d, M, H, A and R are defined above. Rm equals the mortgage rate and H* equals the desired level of housing starts.

Deposit flows to financial institutions (equation 1) are determined by the portfolio decisions of households. Assuming, for the moment no changes in any exogenous variables, as the capital market interest rate increases, deposit flows decrease (disintermediation occurs). The willingness of financial institutions to make mortgage loans (equation 2) depends positively on deposit flows, the level of agency activity and the spread between the mortgage rate and the capital market rate. The demand for mortgage loans by households (equation 3) is a negative function of the mortgage rate and a positive function of housing starts. Incorporated in equation 4 is a disequilibrium effect in the mortgage market. When this market is in equilibrium, Rm clears the market and $M = M^s = M^d$. There have been, however, periods in recent history when the mortgage market has been in disequilibrium due to excess demand. In these instances Rm failed to clear the market, and, thus, $M = M^s < M^d$. Disequilibrium in the mortgage market could also be the result of excess supply in which case M would be equal to M^d but would be less than M^s. As with disequilibrium caused by excess demand, R_m fails to clear the mortgage market if excess supply exists.

If the mortgage market is in equilibrium, the mortgage rate is the key variable in determining the level of housing starts (equation 5). If the market is in disequilibrium, M is the most important determinant of H in equation 5.[2]

Agency activity (equation 6) increases when H < H* and decreases when H > H*.[3] A is also a negative function of deposit flows since FHLB advances and FSCA purchases are viewed by financial institutions as being alternative sources of funds in periods when deposit flows decrease. Agency activities are financed through capital market debt issues. Therefore, an increase in agency activities necessitates additional debt financing and will put upward pressure on the capital market interest rate (equation 7).

Figure 1 may be used to illustrate the effects of agency intervention in periods of mortgage market equilibrium and market disequilibrium. M_0^s is the initial supply schedule and M_0^d is the initial demand schedule. Therefore, Rm* is the initial mortgage rate and M* is the initial quantity of mortgages.

In a period of market equilibrium, an increase in agency activity will shift the supply schedule to the right (to M_1^2). This reduces the mortgage rate (to R_m') which stimulates new housing construction activity (equation 5).

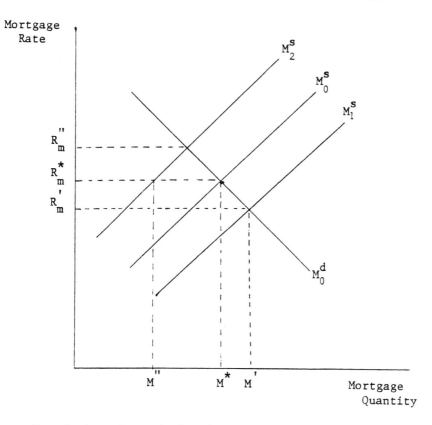

Figure 1. Agency Intervention in Periods of Equilibrium and Disequilibrium

However, as agency activity increases so does the capital market rate (equation 7). As a result the spread between R_m and R will narrow, shifting the supply function to the left (back toward its original position). In addition, as R increases, D will decrease which also pushes M^s back to the left. As M^s moves backward, R_m starts to increase, lowering H.[4]

A period of disequilibrium could occur in the following manner. An exogenous variable (e.g., restrictive monetary policy) raises the capital market rate. As the spread between R_m and R narrows, the mortgage supply schedule starts to shift to the left (to M_2^s). For a variety of reasons, assume that R_m does not rise to its new equilibrium level (R_m''). At R_m^* excess demand exists ($M^* - M''$) and, therefore, the market is in disequilibrium.

As mortgage market activity falls, so will housing market activity (equation 5). Since it is very likely H will fall below the desired level of housing construction activity, agency activity will increase. Agency activity should also increase in response to a drop in savings deposits induced by an increase in R. As in the case when the market is in equilibrium, an increase in A shifts the supply schedule outward, lowering Rm and stimulating H. As before this change is not permanent since an increase in A further increases R, narrowing Rm – R, and so forth.

Agency activity generates increased housing construction activity via different mechanisms depending on the condition of the mortgage market. Under equilibrium conditions, agency activity stimulates housing starts by lowering the mortgage rate. On the other hand, if the market is in disequilibrium, agency activity increases H by increasing the supply of mortgage funds.

A larger rightward shift in the mortgage supply function results, for a given level of agency activity, if the market is in disequilibrium. This is most likely due to the fact that private mortgage lenders will use FHLB advances and FSCA purchases to a greater extent when the market is in disequilibrium. This has two principal implications. First, the same amount of agency activity will generate more housing starts under disequilibrium conditions than it would under equilibrium conditions. Second, agency activity will put more downward pressure on the mortgage rate if the market is in disequilibrium than if it is in equilibrium. By extension, therefore, the drop in the yield spread, Rm – R, will also be greater is excess demand exists in the mortgage market.

Hypotheses

The model illustrates why FSCA secondary mortgage market operations and FHLB advances may have only a temporary impact on the mortgage and housing markets. Several hypotheses may be drawn from this model for more detailed empirical examination. Among these are two which will be examined here. They may be stated as follows:

(1) FHLB and FSCA activities alter the structure of capital market interest rates, lowering the mortgage rate in relation to rates on other long term, fixed income securities (e.g., government and corporate bonds).

(2) As the mortgage rate falls in relation to other market interest rates, private financial institutions respond by reducing their lending activity and/or by making portfolio adjustments (e.g., substituting government bonds for mortgages). Both behavioral changes offset the expansionary effect of FHLB and FSCA activities.

Discussion of Hypothesis I

In recent years, yield spreads between mortgages and other long term fixed-income securities have shown substantial cyclical variation. Illustrated in figure 2 are the yield spreads between mortgages and newly issued A rated utility bonds, and mortgages and treasury bonds from 1971 to 1980.

During this period of time the yield spread between mortgages and treasury bonds averaged 137 basis points (1.37%) ranging from a low of 73 basis points in the second quarter of 1973 to a high of 264 basis points in the fourth quarter of 1974. The yield spread between mortgages and newly

Figure 2.   Yield Spread Between FHA Mortgages and Treasury Bonds, and
Yield Spread Between FHA Mortgages and A Rated Utility Bonds,
from 1971 to 1980
(Source: *Analytical Record of Yields and Spreads*, Salomon
Brothers)

issued A rated utility bonds averaged –31 basis points between 1971 and 1980 ranging from a low of –191 basis points in the second quarter of 1975 to a high of 28 basis points in the third quarter of 1978.

A question raised by these data asks how much of the variation in yield spreads between mortgages and other fixed income securities has been due to the activities of the federal mortgage agencies, and how much has been due to changes in other factors (e.g., risk premiums) which typically account for differences in yields between securities. This question forms the core of Hypothesis I and has been addressed by two empirical studies, Hendershott and Villani (1977) and Jaffee and Rosen (1978).

Hendershott and Villani (1977) specify and empirically estimate equations which model FSCA mortgage purchases, FHLB advances, mortgage demand, housing starts and so forth. These equations, in turn, are used in three simulations which test the effects on the financial markets and housing construction activity of: (1) a freeze on FSCA purchases, (2) a $1 billion one-time purchase of mortgages by FSCAs and (3) changes in the FHLB advance mechanism. One common conclusion from all three simulations is that both FSCA purchases and FHLB advances appear to significantly reduce the mortgage rate vis-à-vis other market interest rates.

In their first simulation, Hendershott and Villani estimate the effects of a freeze on FSCA mortgage purchases at the end of 1965. By the fourth quarter of 1971 the actual mortgage rate was 7.82%. Had a freeze existed, they estimate the mortgage rate would have been 8.88% by the end of 1971. Therefore, FSCA purchases from 1966 to 1971 had the effect of reducing the mortgage rate by 106 basis points. At the same time, Hendershott and Villani also show that a freeze on FSCA purchases would have boasted the corporate bond rate by 19 basis points. Thus, FSCA purchases effectively reduced the yield spread between mortgages and corporate bonds by 87 basis points.

In the second simulation, the effects of a one-time $1 billion purchase by FSCAs (at the beginning of 1969) are measured. Hendershott and Villani estimate that by the end of 1969 this exogenous purchase would have reduced the mortgage rate by 49 basis points. This purchase, they estimate, would have also depressed the corporate bond rate slightly during 1969 (by 3 basis points), thus lowering the yield spread between mortgages and corporate bonds by 46 basis points.

In their final simulation, Hendershott and Villani focus on the impacts of a freeze in FHLB advances at their levels as of the fourth quarter of 1965. They write:

> Observed mortgage rates soared in 1968, rising by a full percentage point. In the absence of new advances they would have averaged 40 basis points more (p. 304).

Similarly, while the observed mortgage rate fell by nearly a full percentage point from mid-1970 to mid-1971, the decline would have been 15 basis points greater had SLAs not repaid advances.

Jaffee and Rosen (1978) provide additional empirical evidence of the impact of FHLB and FSCA activity on the structure of market interest rates. Essentially using the same methodology as Hendershott and Villani, Jaffee and Rosen simulate the impact of an increase in the supply of FSCA purchase commitments during both credit rationing and non-rationing periods.[5]

In the rationing simulation Jaffee and Rosen assume FSCA purchase commitments are increased by $18 billion in September 1974. Four months later, this policy action depressed the mortgage rate by 25.2 basis points, while raising the government bond rate by 18 basis points. In the non-rationing simulation (beginning in April 1976), the same amount of agency commitments lowered the mortgage rate (after 4 months) by 12.4 basis points and raised the government bond rate by 16 basis points.[6]

Model A simulation is one procedure which could be used to test the impact of federal mortgage agency activity on the structure of market interest rates. An alternative procedure, which is a more direct test, develops a model of yield spreads. This model would contain, as explanatory variables, measures of FHLB and FSCA activity as well as other variables commonly used to explain differentials in yields between fixed income securities (default risk, liquidity and the relative level of interest rates). The general regression equation is given below.

$$YS_j = a_0 + a_1FHLB + a_2FSCA + a_3CR + a_4LP + a_5R + e \qquad (8)$$

where YS_j is the yield spread between mortgages and another long term fixed income security, FHLB is the net change in outstanding advances, FSCA is total mortgage purchases by FNMA, GNMA and FHLMC, CR is a measure of default risk premium, LP is a measure of liquidity (or marketability) premium and R is the level of market interest rates. If Hypothesis I is correct both a_1 and a_2 should be negative.

Difference in default risk is another determinant of yield spreads. In general terms, the greater the default risk the higher the yield. In addition, Ferri (1978) and Jaffee (1975) have suggested that yield spreads move in a countercyclical manner to the overall economy, widening when the economy is performing poorly and narrowing in times of economic expansion, apparently because quality differences are more important to investors in periods of economic uncertainty. Past research on yield spread determinants have employed a number of proxies designed to measure default risk. Ferri and Gaines (1980) suggest that the variables representing the risk of default must capture future expectations regarding the course of the economy. As with their study, the index of leading indicators (ILI) will be employed here. It has been documented that the ILI is a good predictor of future turning-points in the economy (e.g., Moore & Shishkin, 1967). If mortgages are more risky than other securities, the default hypothesis suggests that a_3 should be negative; an increase (decrease) in the index decreases (increases) investor fear of default causing them to demand a lower (higher) risk premium on the riskier security.

In general terms, the more liquid a security, the lower its yield. The value in investor places on liquidity may change as market conditions change and the measure of liquidity must be able to reflect these periodic changes. Unfortunately, a host of unobservable expectations (concerning outstanding quantities, future interest rates, etc.) affect an investor's changing appreciation of liquidity. Ferri and Gaines (1980) use the yield spread between treasuries and federal agencies as a proxy for the impact of the differential in liquidity between two securities. Their rationale is based upon the empirical observations of Garbade and Hunt (1978) who showed that the relative illiquidity of agency securities was the prime determinant of the treasury-agency yield spread. At a specific point in time it indicates the premium investors are placing, for whatever complex set of reasons, on increased marketability. This variable will be used as the proxy for the liquidity premium in this study and, as a result, a_4 should be positive.

The last independent variable measures the level of market interest rates. Cook and Hendershott (1978) argue that the level of market interest rates is an important determinant of yield spreads. They argue that a yield spread of 100 basis points is more significant when the market interest rate is 5% than when it is 10%. If a spread is used, including the level of market interest rates as an independent variable will ensure against a situation where an increase in the spread, merely due to increasing interest rates, is not falsely seen as being due to another, more fundamental factor (e.g., an increase in default risk). As a result, it would be expected that a_5 would be positive.

Equation 8 could be specified somewhat differently using a yield ratio as the dependent variable in place of a yield spread. Use of a yield ratio (e.g., YS_j / R_j, where R_j is the jth yield) would eliminate the need for including the level of market interest rates, R, as an additional independent variable in the regression equation.

Yields on three "other" securities will be used to construct yield spreads and ratios in order to test Hypothesis I. They are the yields on: treasury bonds, federal agency bonds and corporate bonds. A total of six regression equations will be estimated.

The model makes two important assumptions. First, it assumes market equilibrium (i.e., $M^d = M^s = M$). This assumption is necessary since it is very difficult to measure and quantify market disequilibrium. Second, the model assumes FHLB and FSCA activities are exogenous to the dependent variables. This assumption is based on empirical studies (e.g., Silber, 1973) which have shown that the federal mortgage agencies respond primarily to the level of housing construction activity and deposit flows, not to the structure of market interest rates.

Discussion of Hypothesis II

The demand for a specific financial asset by a financial institution will depend upon, in part, the set of interest rates relevant for the institution's choice regarding its portfolio composition. If Hypothesis I is correct and, as a consequence of federal mortgage agency activity, mortgages become less attractive investments vis-à-vis other long-term fixed income securities, mortgage lenders should respond by making portfolio adjustments. These adjustments will reduce the effectiveness of federal mortgage agency activity since they offset the initially expansionary impact, on mortgage supply, of FHLB advances and FSCA purchases. This can be seen from the theoretical model (specifically equations 2 and 7).

The composition of financial institutions' portfolios have undergone substantial change in recent years. For some financial institutions, the proportion of their assets invested in mortgages has declined since the mid-1960s. In 1965 mutual savings banks held about 76% of their assets in mortgage loans. By 1970, the proportion of mortgages to total assets had declined to 74%, and currently it is less than 60%. A similar behavior change has also taken place in life insurance companies. Their ratio of mortgages to total assets dropped from over 37% in 1965 to less than 28% today. In savings and loan associations, a non-discretionary lender, mortgages make up a smaller proportion of total assets today (79.8%) than they did in 1965 (85.1%). In fact, of all the major lenders, only commercial banks have increased the percentage of total assets held in mortgage loans since the mid-1960s.[7] After examining these trends, Cook (1974) writes:

> It is highly likely that the main reason for this behavioral change was the substantial decline in the late 1960s of the spread between the mortgage rate and other rates on alternative investments such as corporate bonds (p. 10).

Many empirical studies which have examined the portfolio behavior of financial institutions have used a stock adjustment model to specify "demand" equations for specific financial assets by financial institutions.[8]

A variant of the stock adjustment model states:

$$\Delta X_t = a (X_t^* - X_{t-1}) \tag{10}$$

where, ΔX_t equals the flow into a portfolio of security X during time period t, X_t^* equals the desired level of security X during t, X_{t-1} equals the actual holdings of X at the end of the previous time period $(t-1)$. Finally, a equals a stock adjustment constant $(0 < a < 1)$. Furthermore:

$$X_t^* = f (r, Z) \tag{11}$$

where r is a set of relevant interest rates and Z is a set of non-interest rate variables (e.g., deposit flows) which also determine the desired level of X.

It has been shown by Silver (1970) that interest rate spreads between the various assets are better determinants of asset demand than individual interest rates. Thus equation 11 may be rewritten as:

$$X_t^* = f(YS_j, Z) \tag{12}$$

where YS_j is a set of yield spreads between asset X and other financial assets. In relation to X, these other assets could be either substitutes or complements.[9]

Borrowers will have demand functions for the same financial instruments (viewed by them as liabilities). The same general stock adjustment model (equations 10, 11 and 12) may also be used to specify borrower demand equations for specific financial liabilities. The desired level of liability X (in time period t) will be a function of relative interest rates and several non-interest rate variables.

Using generally the mortgage market model formulated by Rosen and Kearl (1974), the supply of loanable funds (by a financial institution) will be a function of past mortgage commitments, agency activity, deposit flows and relative interest rates. The demand, by borrowers, for loanable funds will be a function of relative interest rates and activity in the housing market.

$$M^d = f(YS, H) \tag{13}$$

$$M^s = f(YS, D, C, A) \tag{14}$$

where YS equals the yield spread between the mortgage rate and the capital market interest rate, D equals deposit flows, C equals past commitments, A equals agency activity and H equals housing market activity.[10]

If hypothesis II is correct, M^s should be positively related to YS. Rosen and Kearl (1974), for example, found that mortgage supply had a significant positive relationship with the spread between the mortgage rate and the AAA corporate bond rate. Silber (1970) found that the supply of mortgage funds by several specific financial institutions depended upon the structure of market interest rates (i.e., the spread between the mortgage rate and the rates on alternative investments.)

There is, however, some ambiguity in the literature concerning the specific portfolio behavior of the largest mortgage lender, savings and loans (SLAs). Silber found that SLAs' lending behavior appeared not to be influenced by the structure of market interest rates. This is perhaps due to the non-discretionary nature of SLAs and statutory restrictions on the composition of their assets. Kent (1981), however, did find that lending behavior by SLAs was, to some extent, influenced by interest rates on alternative investments.

Simple economic theory, confirmed by empirical evidence, suggests that the other non-interest rate determinants should all have positive relationships with mortgage demand and supply. For example, an increase in deposit flows would logically increase the supply of mortgage credit, ceteris paribus.

Model II   Hypothesis II will be tested empirically by constructing and estimating two equations, one representing mortgage supply and the other representing mortgage demand. The equations are given below.

$$\text{demand:}\quad MOR = a_0 + a_1 YS_g + a_2 HS + e_1 \tag{15}$$

$$\text{supply:}\quad MOR = b_0 + b_1 YS_g + b_2 FHLB + b_3 FSCA +$$
$$b_4 DEP + b_5 COM + e_2 \tag{16}$$

where MOR equals the change in mortgage holdings by savings and loan associations, YS_g equals the spread between the mortgage rate and the treasury bond rate (a surrogate for the capital market interest rate), HS equals the dollar value of new homes sold, FHLB equals the net change in FHLB advances, FSCA equals mortgage purchases by FSCAs, DEP equals deposit flows to savings and loans and COM equals outstanding mortgage commitments at savings and loans.

If Hypothesis II is correct, b_1 should be positive. In addition, it is expected that:

$$a_1 < 0 \qquad\qquad b_3 > 0$$

$$a_2 > 0 \qquad\qquad b_4 > 0$$

$$b_2 > 0 \qquad\qquad b_5 > 0.$$

Several comments should be made concerning the specification of equations 15 and 16. First, due to data limitations the model is restricted to savings and loans. Since FSCAs purchase mortgages from all primary lenders, as well as mortgage bankers, this restriction will introduce some measurement error. Second, measurement error will also be introduced due to the fact that savings and loans make mortgage loans on existing as well as new homes while HS is restricted to the value of new homes sold. This restriction is also necessary due to data limitations.

Third, since both equations 15 and 16 share the same dependent variable, MOR, they will be estimated as a system (using second and third stage least squares) as well as individually (using ordinary least squares). Fourth, as with the Hypothesis I model, the Hypothesis II model assumes market equilibrium.

Finally, since the specification of the "price" variable in mortgage demand and supply equations is not clear from the literature, equations 15 and 16 will also be estimated using the mortgage rate, Rm, in place of YSg. When Rm is used, the supply equation will also include the treasury bond rate, Rg, as an additional exogenous variable. Since mortgages and treasury bonds are to some extent substitutes, Rg's coefficient should be negative.

Summary

Chapter 4 introduces a theoretical model which illustrates key relationships among the various market participants. From this model two testable hypotheses are drawn. The first states that FHLB and FSCA activities reduce the mortgage rate in relation to the rates on other, long term fixed income securities. The second hypothesis states that as the mortgage rate falls in relation to other market interest rates, primary mortgage lenders will respond by making portfolio adjustments. These adjustments offset the expansionary impact of FHLB and FSCA activities.

Hypothesis I will be empirically tested by estimating several single equation models of yield spreads. These models include measures of FHLB and FSCA activities as well as other exogenous variables. Hypothesis II will be empirically tested by estimating, using a variety of procedures, a simple model of mortgage demand and supply. Two different "price" variables will be used: the mortgage rate, and the yield spread between mortgages and treasury bonds.

5

Data

This chapter serves two purposes. One, a description of the data series used in this study. Two, a discussion of the seasonality problem, present in most data series, will be presented as well as the procedure used to correct for seasonality.

Description of Data Series

The data series used in this study come from several of public and private sector publications. Two of the most important are the *Federal Reserve Bulletin* and the *Federal Home Loan Bank Board Journal.* These two publications supply FHLB advance and FSCA purchase data as well as data pertaining to savings and loans (deposit flows, outstanding mortgage commitments, and new mortgage loans closed.) The mortgage rate series is also obtained from the *FHLBB Journal.* Other data series are obtained from the *Survey of Current Business* (U.S. Commerce Department), and *An Analytical Record of Yields and Spreads* (Salomon Brothers). Appendix 1 describes each data series in more detail. Data are collected on a monthly basis beginning in January 1972 and ending in December 1980 for a total of 108 observations.

The Problem of Seasonality

Introduction

Seasonality is a widespread phenomenon in economic time series, especially when observations are taken monthly. The failure to adjust for significant seasonal patterns may lead to statistical deficiencies in empirical research.[1] The purpose of this section is to discuss the identification and correction of seasonality in the data series used in this study.

By its very nature, housing construction activity is highly seasonal; the heaviest activity normally occurs during the summer months, the lightest during the winter months. As a result, mortgage market conditions will likely exhibit seasonal fluctuations as well. Therefore, those variables which are closely related to the mortgage market (FSCA purchases, FHLB advances and the mortgage rate) could exhibit seasonality in their behavior over time.[2]

It is also a possibility that the other variables used in this study, which are not as closely related to the housing and mortgage markets may exhibit seasonal patterns as well. For example, Barth and Bennet (1975) and Silber (1970) have shown that market interest rates and the flow of funds to financial institutions, respectively, exhibit characteristics of seasonality.

Seasonality Tests and Adjustments

Several methodologies exist to detect and adjust for seasonality in data series.[3] In this study, the X-11 procedure (as found in the SAS/ETS Library) will be used to remove seasonality from variables where it is determined to be significant. The seasonally adjusted data will then be substituted for the original data when estimating regression equations.

Description of X-11   The X-11 method was developed by the United States Census Bureau. It is based on the assumption that seasonal variation in a data series may be measured and separated from the trend-cycle, trading day and irregular components. Seasonal variation is defined as variation which is repeated constantly, or in an evolving fashion, from year to year. The trend-cycle component includes the long run trend in the data as well as variation due to the business cycle. The trading day component consists of variation due to the fact that some months have fewer days than do other months. The irregular component consists of residual variation.

According to the Census Bureau, experience indicates that many economic time series are related in a multiplicative fashion over time.

$$O = C \times S \times TD \times R \tag{1}$$

where O is the original series, C is the trend-cycle component, S is the seasonal component, TD is the trading day variation component, and R is the residual component.

The X-11 procedure performs three iterations on a data series, each of which provides estimates of seasonal, trend-cycle, trading day and irregular components. During the first iteration, a centered 12 month moving average is applied to the original series to produce a preliminary estimate of the trend-cycle component. Dividing the trend-cycle component into the original series produces an estimate of the seasonal-irregular component (S-I). A weighted moving average is applied to the S-I component to estimate seasonal factors, which are then divided into the S-I series to produce estimates of the irregular component. After adjusting both the seasonal and irregular components for extreme values, a moving average is applied to the modified S-I component in order to produce a preliminary seasonally adjusted series.

Applying a weighted moving average to the seasonally adjusted series produces a new estimate of the trend-cycle curve, and the entire process repeats itself. Each iteration allows the program to make refined estimates of extreme values in the irregular series.[4]

During the final iteration, X-11 performs two tests to attempt to ascertain the significance of seasonal and trading day components. These tests are labeled: trading day regression and stable seasonality test.

Trading Day Regression   Seven daily weights are estimated by regressing the irregular series on the number of times each day of the week occurs during a given month.

$$I_{ij} = a + b_t(D_t) + e_{ij} \tag{2}$$

where I_{ij} equals the irregular value for month j in year i, D_t equals the number of times day t occurs during month j in year i (t = 1, 2, 3, . . . , 7) and e_{ij} is a random error term.

A t statistic is calculated for each coefficient in order to determine its significance. In addition, an overall F test is performed to determine whether or not residual trading day variation is present.[5] If the F test suggests significant trading day variation, at the one percent level, the seven daily weights—derived from regression coefficients—are used to construct monthly factors (i.e., for months with 31 days, 30 days, 29 days and 28 days). These monthly factors are divided into the original series to remove the trading day component.

Stable Seasonality Test   In order to test for the existence of stable seasonality, X-11 computes a one way analysis of variance using the 12 months as treatment groups. The final unmodified S-I ratios are used as observations.

In the ANOVA table, treatment sum of squares is the sum of squares between months, and the error sum of squares is the sum of squares within months. Sum of squares total equals sum of squares between months plus sum of squares within months.[6] The null hypothesis states that the mean S-I ratios are equal for all months and is tested against the alternative that they differ from month to month. Rejection of the null hypothesis is taken as evidence of stable seasonality.

Three points concerning the stable seasonality test should be made.

First, the F test is based on a series of assumptions, and it is possible that several of these assumptions may be violated by the stable seasonality test. However, the F test is relatively robust against violations of its assumptions.[7] Second, X-11 tests only for the existence of stable seasonality. It is possible that if the seasonal component is evolving rapidly enough from year to year, it may not be captured in the between months sum of squares. Thus, a significant seasonal component may go undetected. However, given the time span of this study (9 years), it is unlikely that a seasonal component could evolve rapidly enough not to be at least partly captured by SS (b/m). Finally, X-11 removes the seasonal component even if the null hypothesis cannot be rejected. By contrast, the trading day component is removed only if the trading day F test is significant at the one percent level.

Results

Table 10 presents results of the trading day regressions and stable seasonality tests for the 12 variables used in this study. As the table clearly shows, seasonality is widespread.

Seven of the twelve series contain significant trading day variation at the one percent level. Two of the remaining five series exhibit significant trading day variation at the five percent level. Evidence of stable seasonality,

Table 10. Principal Results of
Trading Day Regressions and
Stable Seasonality Tests

| | F Statistics | |
Variable	Trading Day	Stable Seasonality
LIQ	3.268**	1.254
ILI	1.985	8.230**
Rm	3.969**	8.448**
Rg	2.708*	3.381**
Rc	.614	1.203
Rab	4.997**	2.233*
FHLB	2.133	8.522**
FSCA	2.507*	5.070**
DEP	5.196**	33.396**
MOR	18.635**	21.267**
COMM	1.349	23.073**
HS	6.207**	40.105**

* - significant at .05 level
** - significant at .01 level

Table 11. Descriptive Statistics of Adjusted Variables

Variable	Mean	St. Dev.	Min.	(Date)	Max.	(Date)
FHLB[1]	404.70	659.99	−1205.17	(3/73)	3510.19	(3/80)
FSCA[1]	1007.61	451.66	253.74	(1/77)	1970.41	(8/78)
ILI	129.07	9.36	106.72	(2/75)	143.80	(10/78)
LIQ[2]	3.88	22.92	− 72.93	(6/74)	58.53	(7/72)
YS1[3]	1.675	.334	.002	(2/80)	2.334	(12/76)
YS2	.242	.063	− .0001	(2/80)	.362	(8/72)
YS3[3]	1.249	.406	.042	(2/80)	2.009	(12/76)
YS4	.170	.062	.004	(2/80)	.296	(12/76)
YS5[3]	− .106	.479	− 1.509	(2/80)	.806	(8/79)
YS6	− .013	.051	− .133	(2/80)	.077	(7/79)
MOR[1]	6027.71	2310.39	2339.86	(11/74)	9779.12	(12/77)
DEP[1]	2977.16	1365.04	− 918.77	(8/74)	6113.36	(4/75)
COMM[1]	15540.97	4636.32	8694.85	(11/74)	22689.05	(12/77)
HS[1]	2491.77	937.61	1176.21	(12/74)	4189.72	(10/78)

[1] - Millions of dollars
[2] - Basis points
[3] - Percent

at the one percent level, is found in all but three variables. One of the three, the agency bond rate, exhibits stable seasonality at the five percent level. Of the twelve variables, only the corporate bond rate, Rc, exhibits neither stable seasonality nor trading day variation.

Conclusion

Given the test results generated by the X-11 program, seasonally adjusted data (i.e., with only the trend-cycle and residual components remaining) will be substituted for original data for 11 of the 12 variables in the regression models, results of which will be reported in the following chapter. Descriptive statistics of the variables are presented in table 11.

6

Empirical Results

This chapter will report on the findings of the empirical tests of the two hypotheses which constitute this study. These hypotheses were developed in chapter 4.

Hypothesis One

Hypothesis one states that a consequence of FHLB advance activity and FSCA purchase activity is a reduction in the mortgage rate relative to the rates on other, long term, fixed income securities. This hypothesis is tested by estimating six single equation regression models where the dependent variable is either a yield spread (e.g., Rm − Rg) or a yield ratio (e.g., (Rm − Rg)/Rg). Regressors include measures of FHLB and FSCA activities as well as measures of default risk and illiquidity risk.

Ordinary Least Squares Results

The argument that FHLB and FSCA activities tend to reduce the mortgage rate in relation to other market interest rates appears to be generally supported by the results. As indicated in table 12, all FSCA and FHLB coefficients have the correct sign, negative, and most are statistically significant at the one percent level. Relationships are generally stronger in those equations where a yield ratio is used as the dependent variable (equations 4, 5, and 6) as measured by respective t statistics.

Therefore, it can be tentatively concluded that a significant amount of the variation in yield spreads and ratios between mortgages and other financial instruments may be explained by variations in FHLB and FSCA activities.

The results, however, also suggest that the relative impacts of FHLB and FSCA activities on yield spreads and ratios may not be that large. Table 13 gives the elasticities (at the means) of the FHLB and FSCA coefficients. These elasticities indicate that in many instances, a large increase in agency

Table 12.   Hypothesis I:
Ordinary Least Squares Estimates

Model	1	2	3
Dependent variable	YS1	YS3	YS5
Intercept	1.5468	-3.1287	-6.3297
FHLB	-.0033	-.0004	-.0002
	(5.5240)	(6.3868)	(4.6237)
FSCA	-.0001	-.0003	-.0002
	(1.0386)	(3.0440)	(2.4422)
CR	.0049	.0368	-.0551
	(1.2616)	(7.7021)	(12.9105)
LP	-.0012	.0019	-.0018
	(.9449)	(1.2680)	(1.3529)
R	-.0390	.0205	-.0494
	(1.0527)	(.4528)	(1.2214)
R^2	.4712	.4658	.6942
MSE	.0620	.0927	.0740
D-W	.9735	1.0202	.5837

Model	4	5	6
Dependent variable	YS2	YS4	YS6
Intercept	.2501	-.3869	-.6716
FHLB	-.00050	-.00060	-.00002
	(6.7480)	(5.0158)	(3.7106)
FSCA	-.00007	-.00008	-.00003
	(7.4411)	(5.6331)	(4.2024)
CR	.00067	.00520	-.00559
	(1.1987)	(7.9363)	(12.8372)
LP	-.00190	.00034	-.00021
	(1.0846)	(1.6687)	(1.3827)
R^2	.6927	.5594	.6917
MSE	.0013	.0018	.0008
D-W	1.1324	1.1848	.5340

Note: t statistic given below coefficient estimate in parentheses.

activities will produce only a modest decrease in yield spreads and ratios. For example, a $100 million increase in FHLB advances will only reduce the mortgage-treasury and mortgage-corporate yield spreads by about 80 and 50 basis points respectively.

The other independent variables produce mixed results. In some cases coefficients lack statistical significance and/or have the wrong sign. Some results are, in retrospect, not surprising. For example, results from equations 3 and 6 suggest that corporate bonds are viewed as having more default risk than mortgages, as the yield spread between mortgages and corporate bonds

Table 13.   Elasticities of Policy Variables*

Model	Uncorrected Models**		Corrected Models**	
	FHLB	*FSCA*	*FHLB*	*FSCA*
1	–.797	–.060	–.024	.018
2	–.130	–.339	–.067	–.208
3	–.506	–1.765	–.065	–.081
4	–.836	–.409	–.952	–.356
5	–1.428	–.665	–.076	.441
6	–.623	–2.325	–.311	–.775

*At means.
**Uncorrected or corrected for autoregressive disturbances.

narrows as economic conditions worsen. The measure of the corporate bond rate consisted of the average yield on corporate bonds with ratings from AAA to BBB. In light of the above, this result is not unexpected.

The estimates of a_4, the coefficient for the measure of illiquidity premiums, have the wrong signs in many models and are also not statistically significant. This raises two questions. First, perhaps mortgages and these other financial instruments do not differ significantly in terms of liquidity (which seems unlikely) or second, perhaps the illiquidity measure used here, a federal agency–treasury yield spread, is a poor proxy.

Some studies which use yield spreads as independent variables transform the raw monthly data into centered three month moving averages. This is done in order to remove transient components from the yield spread (e.g., the temporary impacts of relative supplies).[1]

Serial Correlation

Ordinary least squares makes several important assumptions about the data used. One of these is that the error term exhibits no serial correlation, Cov $(e_t, e_{t-j}) = 0$, where $j \neq 0$.

If this assumption is violated, and it frequently is when time series data are used, the estimates of the regression coefficients are still unbiased and consistent. However, they are neither efficient nor asymptotically efficient. As a result, the standard error of a regression coefficient may be smaller than its "true" value. In addition, the calculated mean square error (MSE) may seriously underestimate the true value of the error variance (σ^2).

Identification of Serial Correlation   If serial correlation does exist, Kmenta (1971) suggests that the error term most frequently follows an autoregressive process.

$$e_t = \rho_1 e_{t-1} + \rho_2 e_{t-2} + \ldots + \rho_n e_{t-n} + u_t \qquad (1)$$

where u_t is a normally and independently distributed random variable with a mean of zero and a constant variance. The autoregressive parameters, ρ_j, have values between positive and negative one.

Examining the autocorrelation function (ACF) and partial autocorrelation function (PACF) for e_t often sheds light on the order of the autoregressive process, if one exists at all.[2] This was done for all six equations and results suggest the existence of first order autoregressive schemes (i.e., $e_t = \rho e_{t-1} + u_t$). The existence of first order autoregression was also suggested by results of the Durbin-Watson test. The D-W statistic for each equation is given in table 12. All are significant at the five percent level.[3]

Correcting for Serial Correlation Several methods, with varying degrees of complexity, may be used to compensate for first order autoregressive disturbances. The most common methods are discussed by Kmenta (1971, pp. 282-92). The method used here is an iterative procedure used by the SAS Autoreg program. Essentially, the program calculates preliminary estimates of the autoregressive parameters from the residuals of the OLS regression. The parameters are used to transform the original data and then, using the transformed data, regression coefficients are re-estimated using OLS. The process is repeated until the estimates converge.

Parameter estimates are usually similar to those produced by OLS, although they may be smaller. However, the standard errors may be quite different, affecting significance tests. The coefficient of determination, R^2, should also fall once the model is adjusted.

Adjusted Results Presented in table 14 are major results of the six regression equations after adjustment for first order autocorrelation.

A comparison of tables 12 and 14 indicates that the parameter estimates, for the most part, are slightly smaller and usually retain the same sign. However, standard errors and R^2 values do change. In most cases the standard error increases resulting in a decrease in the corresponding t statistic. In equations 1, 2 and 3 the significance of FHLB and FSCA activities are reduced, in some cases below the five percent level. However, in equations 4, 5 and 6 parameter estimates of agency activities retain their statistical significance. Along with the size of the coefficient, elasticities fall as well. For example, before correcting for autocorrelation, $100 million in FHLB advances would reduce YS1 by about 80 basis points—after correcting for autocorrelation $100 million in advances reduces YS1 by less than three basis points. The elasticities are presented in table 13.

The coefficient of determination, for an equation, will fall in relation to

Table 14. Hypothesis I: Estimates Corrected for
Autoregressive Disturbances

Model	1	2	3
Dependent variable	YS1	YS3	YS3
Intercept	3.00324	−1.13466	−3.99361
FHLB	−.00010	−.00022	−.00003
	(2.376)	(3.717)	(.673)
FSCA	.00003	−.00013	.00007
	(.333)	(.936)	(.211)
CR	−.00140	.02533	−.04489
	(.277)	(4.239)	(7.686)
LP	−.00132	.00003	−.00083
	(1.212)	(.023)	(.968)
R	−.15602	−.09592	−.25539
	(3.478)	(1.801)	(5.434)
R^2	.3350	.2913	.4747
MSE	.0395	.0596	.0264
$\hat{\rho}$	.5105	.4780	.7042

Model	4	5	6
Dependent variable	YS2	YS4	YS6
Intercept	.38429	−.22701	−.49418
FHLB	−.00004	−.00042	−.00001
	(5.023)	(4.990)	(2.398)
FSCA	−.00005	−.00006	−.00001
	(4.534)	(4.291)	(1.636)
CR	−.00062	.00367	.00401
	(.784)	(4.556)	(6.076)
LP	−.00027	.00001	−.00009
	(1.639)	(.038)	(1.552)
R^2	.5001	.3661	.3053
MSE	.0009	.0013	.0003
$\hat{\rho}$	.4297	.3869	.7318

Note: t statistic given below coefficient estimate in parentheses.

the estimated value of ρ. In the equation with the largest $\hat{\rho}$, equation 6, R^2 falls from .534 to .305.

In conclusion, the empirical results provide some evidence in support of hypothesis one, although the impact of agency activity on market interest rates appears to be relatively small. While hypothesis one is not as strongly supported after the equations are corrected for serial correlation, the results still provide some evidence in support of it.

Hypothesis Two

Hypothesis two states that primary mortgage lenders respond to changes in market interest rates by making portfolio adjustments. Thus as the mortgage rate falls relative to other market interest rates, the level of new mortgage lending activity should fall as well. It is this reduction in lending activity which will reduce the expansionary effect of FHLB and FSCA activities.

Two equations constitute hypothesis two. The first measures mortgage demand and the second measures mortgage supply. Both equations share the same dependent variable, the volume of new residential mortgage loans issued by savings and loan associations.

Three methods are used to estimate the two equations. In addition to ordinary least squares, two stage least squares (2SLS) and three stage least squares (3SLS) are used. The latter two procedures assume the equations form an interrelated system.

Two different "price" variables are used: the yield spread between mortgages and government bonds (YS1) and the mortgage rate (Rm). In the cases where Rm is used, Rg (government bond rate) is included as an additional exogenous variable in the supply equation. Since government bonds and mortgages may be viewed by savings and loans as substitutes, the coefficient should be negative.

OLS Results

Ordinary least squares estimates of the demand and supply equations are presented in table 15. In general, with both price variables, hypothesis two appears to be weakly supported; while the coefficients have the correct sign, neither are statistically significant. All other coefficients have the hypothesized signs, the only exception being FSCA's coefficient, and most are statistically significant.

Results of the Durbin-Watson test indicate the presence of first order autoregressive disturbances. Revised estimates, after the data are adjusted, are presented in table 16. Some parameter estimates change as do most of the standard errors. Perhaps most interesting is that hypothesis two appears to be more strongly supported after adjustment, judged by the respective t statistics.

System Estimates

The two equations which constitute hypothesis two can be viewed as forming a simple system of equations. As Kmenta points out, using ordinary least squares to estimate a portion of a system may produce inconsistent estimators of regression coefficients.

In particular, when a relation is part of a system, some regressors are typically stochastic and correlated with the regression disturbances. In this case the ordinary least squares estimators of the regression coefficients are not consistent (p. 531).

Description of a System A system consists of predetermined variables—variables determined primarily outside the system—and variables determined primarily by the system. They are called exogenous and endogenous variables respectively. In this system, MOR (quantity of new mortgage loans) and the price variable (YS1 or Rm) are endogenous while the other variables (HS, FHLB, FSCA, DEP, COMM, and Rg) are exogenous. This model, therefore, can be seen as constituting a system of simultaneous equations.[4]

Structural and Reduced Form Equations In this model, the structural equations (using YS1 as the price variable) are:

$$\text{demand:} \quad \text{MOR} = a_0 + a_1\text{YS1} + a_2\text{HS} + e_1 \tag{2}$$

$$\text{supply:} \quad \text{MOR} = b_0 + b_1\text{YS1} + b_2\text{FHLB} + b_3\text{FSCA} + b_4\text{COMM}$$
$$+ b_5\text{DEP} + e_2 \tag{3}$$

Reduced form equations, where endogenous variables are stated only in terms of exogenous variables are:

$$\text{MOR} = c_{11} + c_{12}\text{HS} + c_{13}\text{FHLB} + c_{14}\text{FSCA} + c_{15}\text{COMM}$$
$$+ c_{16}\text{DEP} + v_1 \tag{4}$$

$$\text{YS1} = c_{21} + c_{22}\text{HS} + c_{23}\text{FHLB} + c_{24}\text{FSCA} + c_{25}\text{COMM}$$
$$+ c_{26}\text{DEP} + v_2 \tag{5}$$

The reduced form equations show explicitly how endogenous variables are jointly dependent on exogenous variables and residuals of the system. Appendix 2 shows how the reduced form equations are derived from the structural equations.

Identification of Structural Equations The identification issue is more mathematical than statistical, yet it has important implications for the alternative methods of estimating regression parameters. Simply stated, the identification issue seeks to determine whether the reduced form parameters can be used to deduce unique estimates of the structural parameters. In other words, is it possible to state the a's and b's in terms of the c's? If there is a unique solution for restricted parameters (a's and b's) in terms of the unrestricted parameters (c's), exact identification exists. If there is no unique solution, overidentification exists. Finally, if the number of unrestricted parameters is not sufficient for solution, underidentification exists. An equation is said to be identified if it is either overidentified or exactly identified.

Identification of the equations may be ascertained by substituting for MOR and YS1 from the reduced form equations into the structural equations. As shown in appendix 3, the demand equation is overidentified and the supply equation is exactly identified. Thus, both equations are identified.

Two Stage Least Square Results   Two stage least square is a single equation method of estimation (i.e., each equation is estimated separately) and thus in one respect is similar to ordinary least squares. However, 2SLS differs from OLS because it takes into account the effect, on the equation being estimated, of all exogenous variables, even those which appear elsewhere in the model.

As can be seen from the structural equations, the price variable is not

Table 15. Hypotheses II:
Uncorrected Estimates

| | Demand Equation Estimation Procedure | | |
	OLS	2SLS	3SLS
Intercept	-276.220	-617.654	-617.654
HS	2.364	2.376	2.376
	(30.974)	(30.562)	(30.562)
YS1	246.128	433.263	433.263
	(1.147)	(1.402)	(1.402)
R^2	.9105	.9099	*
MSE	487.730	491,600	**
D-W	.5203	.5364	—
Intercept	3,123.086	3,340.832	3,340.832
HS	2.628	2.649	2.649
	(30.780)	(30.473)	(30.473)
Rm	-412.059	-442.471	-442.471
	(5.237)	(5.384)	(5.384)
R^2	.9294	.9294	*
MSE	384,510	385,140	**
D-W	.7682	.7778	—

Table 15. Continued

	Supply Equation Estimation Procedure		
	OLS	*2SLS*	*3SLS*
Intercept	−1,953.231	−6,875.436	−13,972.302
YS1	179,517	2,928,223	7,080.480
	(.882)	(1.635)	(4.313)
FHLB	.069	.984	2.102
	(.538)	(1.574)	(3.773)
FSCA	−.257	.378	1.772
	(1.775)	(.792)	(4.151)
COMM	.469	.412	.316
	(26.548)	(8.627)	(7.433)
DEP	.229	.262	.211
	(4.556)	(2.908)	(2.635)
R^2	.9583	.8836	*
MSE	234,390	712,600	**
D-W	.5603	.8893	—
Intercept	−1,168.243	−6,856.829	−10,744.001
Rm	102.618	2,797.734	4,775.224
	(.499)	(1.981)	(3.511)
FHLB	.094	.899	1.396
	(.746)	(1.946)	(3.137)
FSCA	−.075	.243	.698
	(.428)	(.721)	(2.154)
COMM	.473	.414	.381
	(26.853)	(9.723)	(9.041)
DEP	.232	.258	.214
	(4.682)	(3.028)	(2.610)
Rg	−233.016	−2,736.472	−4,615.567
	(1.148)	(2.078)	(3.636)
R^2	.9598	.8930	*
MSE	228,630	656,890	**
D-W	.8250	.8509	—

Note: t statistic given below coefficient estimate in parentheses.
*Weighted R^2 for system equals .9465.
**Weighted MSE for system equals .5424.

truly exogenous. The 2SLS procedure first estimates the reduced form price equation (number 5) and produces values for YŜ1—the value of YS1 predicted from all exogenous variables. Then each structural equation is estimated with YŜ1 replacing YS1.

Principal 2SLS results are presented in table 15. In general, the results tend to provide stronger support for hypothesis two than the OLS results do.

However, YS1's coefficient in the demand equation has the wrong sign. In addition, all exogenous variables have the correct sign and most are statistically significant. Equations which used Rm as the price variable tend to produce somewhat better results, judged by respective t statistics and R^2 values.

The D-W statistics indicate the presence of first order autoregressive disturbances. Using a procedure similar to the one described by Kmenta (pp. 587–89), adjusted estimates are obtained. These results are presented in table 16. After adjustment, the results do not as strongly support hypothesis two. However, the price coefficients still have the correct signs, as do most of the exogenous variables. In addition, most coefficients are still statistically significant at the five percent level. As expected, R^2 falls in relation to the size of the autoregression coefficient.

Three Stage Least Squares Results   Two stage least squares estimates are an improvement over ordinary least squares estimates in that 2SLS estimators are consistent. However, since 2SLS is a single equation method of estimation, it disregards the possibility of correlation among the errors across equations. Since it fails to use all available information, 2SLS estimators may not be asymptotically efficient.

Table 16.   Hypotheses II:
Estimates Corrected for
Autoregressive Disturbances

| | Demand Equation Estimation Procedure | | |
	OLS	*2SLS*	*3SLS*
Intercept	434.677	1,645.626	1,645.626
HS	1.804	1.733	1.733
	(12.386)	(7.168)	(7.168)
YS1	−90.295	−2,523.001	−2,523.001
	(.443)	(2.901)	(2.890)
R^2	.620	.426	*
MSE	197,050	491,940	**
Intercept	316.894	513.132	513.132
HS	1.989	2.028	2.028
	(13.056)	(12.822)	(12.822)
Rm	13.244	−64.416	−64.416
	(.098)	(.404)	(.404)
R^2	.6919	.6993	*
MSE	206,780	207.480	**

Table 16. Continued

| | Supply Equation Estimation Procedure | | |
	OLS	2SLS	3SLS
Intercept	−534.181	−1,344.980	−777.853
YS1	320.017	1,810.467	625.436
	(2.187)	(1.114)	(.396)
FHLB	.367	.549	.402
	(4.804)	(2.425)	(1.857)
FSCA	−.206	−.112	−.287
	(1.581)	(.520)	(1.406)
COMM	.471	.501	.496
	(19.343)	(10.394)	(10.347)
DEP	.032	.016	.042
	(.968)	(.224)	(.632)
R²	.8339	.7013	*
MSE	89,045	189,490	**
Intercept	−495.623	−1,960.320	4,832.608
Rm	275.103	1,588.513	4,202.198
	(1.596)	(1.457)	(4.160)
FHLB	.359	.397	.339
	(4.280)	(3.554)	(3.355)
FSCA	−.179	−.255	.300
	(1.272)	(1.340)	(1.749)
COMM	1.478	.470	.413
	(20.578)	(15.376)	(14.223)
DEP	.046	.007	.081
	(1.345)	(.124)	(1.641)
Rg	−346.129	−1,293.770	−3,113.090
	(2.264)	(1.627)	(4.209)
R²	.8639	.7952	*
MSE	95,316	156,090	**

Note: t statistic given below coefficient estimate in parentheses.
*Weighted R² for system equals .7626
**Weight MSE for system equals .6809.

Three stage least squares is one of several system methods of estimation. System procedures estimate all regression parameters of the structural equations together as a set and thus use all available information. Essentially 3SLS is an extension of 2SLS, residuals from the second stage estimates are used to compute a contemporaneous variance—covariance matrix of the equation's residuals. Generalized least squares is then used to produce simultaneous estimates of all model parameters.

Two points concerning 3SLS should be made. First, if the residuals are not correlated across equations, third stage estimates will be identical to second stage estimates. Second, Zellner and Theil (1962) have shown that the omission of exactly identified equations will not affect the third stage estimates of the remaining equations. Thus, exactly identified equations add no information for estimating overidentified equations. Since the reverse is not true, the third stage estimates of the demand equation will be identical to the second stage estimates, but the third stage estimates of the supply equation may differ from the second stage estimates.

Results of the third stage least squares procedure are presented in table 15 (unadjusted for serial correlation) and table 16 (adjusted for serial correlation). Hypothesis two is strongly supported by the unadjusted estimates. In addition, the overall estimation of the supply equation conforms to the hypothesized format, all of the coefficients have the correct sign and are statistically significant. After adjustment, the results are not as good; some coefficients are incorrectly signed and/or not statistically significant. YS1's coefficient in the supply equation is no longer statistically significant although it retains the correct sign. On the other hand, the coefficient of Rm is correctly signed and significant.

Elasticity of Price Variables

Elasticities (at the means) of the price variables from the supply equations are presented in table 17 for each estimation procedure uncorrected and corrected for autoregressive disturbances. The elasticities suggest that relatively large changes in the mortgage rate and the mortgage-treasury yield spread are necessary to induce modest changes in the supply of mortgage loans issued by savings and loans. For example, from models corrected for autocorrelation, elasticities for Rm range from .3753 to 5.734 indicating that

Table 17.   Elasticities of Price Variables
from Supply Equations*

| Estimation | Uncorrected** | | Corrected** | |
Procedure	YS1	Rm	YS1	Rm
OLS	.0499	.1405	.0889	.3754
2SLS	.8137	3.8292	.5081	2.1676
3SLS	1.9675	6.5357	.1738	5.7340

*At means.
**Uncorrected or corrected for autoregressive disturbances.

a one percent decrease in the mortgage rate would reduce the supply of mortgage loans by .375% to 5.734%. As with hypothesis one, elasticities are generally smaller after corrections for autoregressive disturbances are made.

Conclusion

Chapter 6 has presented the principal empirical findings on the two hypotheses which form the core of this study. Hypothesis one was tested by estimating six single equation models of yield spreads and yield ratios using ordinary least squares. Without correcting for serial correlation, results suggest FHLB and FSCA activities depress the mortgage rate in relation to other market interest rates. The results, however, indicate that large increases in agency activities are necessary to induce relatively small changes in yield spreads and yield ratios. After correction for serial correlation, the evidence is not as conclusive, but some support for hypothesis one remains.

The two equations which constitute hypothesis two were estimated using three procedures (ordinary least squares, two stage least squares and three stage least squares) with two different price variables (YS1 and Rm). The majority of the results, tend to support the argument that mortgage lenders make portfolio adjustments in response to changes in market interest rates. These adjustments are in the form of a reduction in the amount of new mortgage loans made. However, the results also suggest large changes in relative interest rates are necessary before large changes in lending volume occur. As with hypothesis one, the strength of the support for hypothesis two is not as strong, in general, once the data are corrected for serial correlation, but evidence in support of the hypothesis remains.

7

Conclusions

This study set out to provide empirical evidence of one possible explanation Cook (1974) raised concerning the long term ineffectiveness of federal mortgage policy to meet its principal policy objectives: to increase and stabilize the availability of residential mortgage credit. The existing literature suggests that while FHLB advances and FSCA secondary mortgage market operations have some significant short term effects on the housing and mortgage markets, their activities are relatively ineffective in the long run.

In order to accomplish this objective, a theoretical model of the housing and mortgage markets was developed. From this model, two testable hypotheses were drawn. The first hypothesis stated that actions by federal mortgage agencies tended to reduce the mortgage rate in relation to the rates on other long term, fixed income securities. The second hypothesis, in part based on the first, stated that primary mortgage lenders respond to changes in the structures of market interest rates by making portfolio adjustments which counteract the expansionary impact of FHLB and FSCA activities.

The first hypothesis was tested by constructing and estimating single equation models of yield spreads and yield ratios. Six equations were estimated examining yield spreads (and ratios) between mortgages and treasury, federal agency and corporate bonds. Independent variables included measures of federal agency activity as well as other determinants of yield spreads (default and illiquidity premiums).

The major results with respect to hypothesis one are summarized in table 18. While support for the hypothesis is somewhat ambiguous—in some models regression coefficients have the wrong sign and/or are not statistically significant—in general the results suggest that FHLB and FSCA activities induce changes in the structure of market interest rates. However, the impact of FHLB and FSCA activities on yield spreads and ratios appears to be quite small. The elasticity measures show that large changes in the level of FHLB and FSCA activities are necessary to induce only modest changes in the structure of interest rates. For example, the results indicate that a $100

Table 18.   Hypotheses I: Summary of Results[1]

| | Policy Variable[2] | | | |
| | FHLB | | FSCA | |
Yield Spread[2]	Statistical Significance	Elasticity at Means	Statistical Significance	Elasticity of Means
YS1	**	−.0242	NS	.0180
YS2	**	−.0669	**	−.2082
YS3	**	−.0648	NS	−.0807
YS4	**	−.9522	**	−.3556
YS5	NS	−.0759	NS	.4408
YS6	**	−.3113	*	−.7751

1. From models corrected for autoregressive disturbances.
2. See Appendix 1 for definitions of policy variables and yield spreads.
**Significant at 1% level.
*Significant at 5% level.
NS—Not significant at 5% level.

million increase in FHLB advances will reduce the mortgage-treasury yield spread by less than three basis points.

Hypothesis two involved the construction of mortgage demand and supply equations. In both equations the dependent variable was new mortgage loans closed at savings and loan associations. Two different "price" variables were used (the mortgage-treasury yield spread, and the mortgage rate). Price variables were included in both equations along with exogenous determinants of mortgage demand and supply. The equations were estimated using three procedures: ordinary least squares, two stage least square and three stage least squares.

Principal results with respect to hypothesis two are presented in table 19. As with the first hypothesis, while support for hypothesis two is not overwhelming, in general, the results do suggest that mortgage lending behavior of savings and loan associations is a function of the structure of market interest rates. However, the results also suggest that relatively large changes in interest rates are necessary to induce major changes in lending behavior.

Public Policy Implications and Topics for Future Research

Despite the ambiguous nature of results of this study, questions are nonetheless raised about the effectiveness of federal mortgage policy at meeting its principal stated objectives: to stabilize and increase the availability of mortgage credit allowing housing to obtain a larger and more stable

Table 19. Hypothesis II: Summary of Results[1]

| | Mortgage Price Variable[2] | | | |
| | YS1 | | RM | |
Estimation Procedure	*Statistical Significance*	*Elasticity at Mean*	*Statistical Significance*	*Elasticity at Mean*
Ordinary least squares	*	.0889	NS	.3754
Two stage least squares	NS	.5081	NS	2.1676
Three stage least squares	NS	.1738	**	5.7340

1. From supply equations adjusted for autoregressive disturbances.
2. See Appendix 1 for definitions of price variables.
**Significant at 1% level.
*Significant at 5% level
NS—Not significant at 5% level.

share of GNP. If FHLB and FSCA activities alter the structure of interest rates leading to offsetting reactions by private market participants, should their activities be changed or even scaled back? On the other hand, what would be the consequence to the housing and home finance industries if FHLB and FSCA activities were changed or scaled back? These questions, at the present time, cannot be definitively answered. Therefore, it would appear that more research into a variety of topics is necessary. These topics include: an examination of pass-through securities issued by GNMA and FHLMC and an examination of other possible effects (aside from the credit availability question) of FHLB and FSCA activities.

In 1979 new pass-through securities issued or backed by GNMA and FHLMC totaled $24.0 billion. This figure represented over five percent of total funds raised in U.S. credit markets during all of 1979. In addition, GNMA and FHLMC pass-through securities are the fastest growing type of federal mortgage agency activity. A major question with respect to pass-through securities is: do primary mortgage lenders substitute pass-through securities for direct mortgage lending? The existing empirical evidence is not clear. A recent study by Wachtel (1981) found evidence that mutual savings banks have to some extent substituted GNMA pass-through securities for direct mortgage lending. However, another study, Seiders (1979), found that a large portion of pass-through securities were purchased by institutional investors not normally involved in direct mortgage lending (e.g., life insurance companies and pension funds). The major rationale behind GNMA and FHLMC pass-through securities is that they tap essentially new sources of capital for the mortgage market. Therefore, evidence of portfolio substitution similar to what Wachtel found would be contrary to this rationale.

The literature has extensively examined the question of the effectiveness of FHLB and FSCA actions at meeting their primary policy objectives. However, there have been few attempts to examine other, perhaps beneficial, effects of agency activities. For example, has the development of a federally sponsored secondary mortgage market improved the liquidity of primary mortgage lenders? Has the secondary market helped to improve the flow of funds from capital surplus regions of the country to capital deficit regions? Aside from the credit availability question it is possible that the federal mortgage agencies have improved the overall efficiency and functioning of the mortgage market.

Federal Mortgage Policy and the Future

Aside from questions concerning their effectiveness and their proper role in the housing and mortgage markets, the future of the federal mortgage agencies will doubtlessly be affected by larger political and economic changes. One of these is a growing debate among policy makers as to the proper amount of GNP which should be devoted to housing.

Since the 1930s a fundamental tenet of public policy is that housing should obtain a large and stable share of GNP. In recent years this tenet has come under more and more scrutiny. Some argue that housing, partly due to preferential treatment by government, has today obtained too large a share of GNP and, by extension, too large a proportion of loanable funds is siphoned off for residential mortgage loans. The result of this, it is argued, is that less funds are available for other, more productive sectors of the economy and this is one cause of sluggish economic growth. Others argue quite the opposite. Housing, they insist, is a key industry for both economic and social reasons, and even a larger share of GNP should be devoted to it. They argue that a large and healthy housing sector is not the cause of economic problems but rather a solution to them.

There can be little argument, however, that a large portion of the total funds raised each year in the U.S. credit markets flows into the mortgage market. For example, in 1979 private mortgage lenders made a total of $113.7 billion in residential mortgage loans. This figure represented 24.1 percent of the total amount raised in U.S. credit markets during 1979. In addition, the federal mortgage agencies raised over $25 billion in the money and capital markets in 1979 and issued another $24 billion in mortgage pass-through securities. Whether or not too much flows, directly or indirectly, into the mortgage market is not a question to be answered here. However, the resolution of this fundamental question will profoundly affect the future course of FHLB and FSCA activities.

Also changing is the structure and functions of financial institutions. It is possible that some of these changes could reduce the need for federal mortgage agencies in the future. One example is the trend towards larger, more consolidated financial institutions. These new institutions may be able to directly tap the credit markets for funds in much the same way federal mortgage agencies do today. Even today some larger financial institutions and home builders are issuing their own mortgage backed securities to raise funds for home loans. If mortgage lending financial institutions need to rely less on short term deposits as their primary source of funds, perhaps the need for FHLB and FSCA activities will be reduced in the future.

Regardless of how these and other questions are resolved, federal mortgage agency activity will remain highly significant in the future. Their activities will still have a great deal of impact on not only the housing and mortgage markets, but the overall economy as well. Thus, a better understanding of these activities and their consequences should lead to the better overall formulation of public policy.

Appendix 1

Description of Data Series

Variable	Description and Source
FHLB	Net change in FHLB advances. Source: *Federal Home Loan Bank Board Journal.*
FSCA	Total purchases by FNMA, FHLMC and GNMA. Source: *Federal Reserve Bulletin.*
MOR	New residential mortgage loans closed at savings and loan associations. Source: *FHLB Journal.*
DEP	Net deposit flows to savings and loans. Source: *FHLB Journal.*
COMM	Outstanding residential mortgage loan commitments at savings and loans. Source: *FHLB Journal.*
HS	Total value of new housing units sold. Source: *Construction Reports*, U.S. Census Bureau.
ILI	Index of leading economic indicators. Source: *Business Conditions Digest*, U.S. Commerce Department.
LIQ	Yield spread between one year federal agency bonds and one year Treasury bonds. Source: *Analytical Record of Yields and Yield Spreads*, Salomon Brothers.
Rm	Effective yield on new residential mortgage loans. Source: *FHLB Journal.*
Rg	Average yield on long term Treasury bonds. Source: *Federal Reserve Bulletin.*
Rab	Average yield on long term federal agency bonds. Source: *Analytical Record of Yields and Yield Spreads.*
Rc	Average yield on long term corporate bonds with ratings of Aaa, Aa, A and Baa. Source: *Federal Reserve Bulletin.*

Appendix 2

Structural and Reduced Form Equations

The following two equations, using YS1 as the price variable, constitute hypothesis II.

$$MOR = a_0 + a_1YS1 + a_2HS + e_1 \tag{1}$$

$$MOR = b_0 + b_1YS1 + b_2FHLB + b_3FSCA + b_4COMM + b_5DEP + e_2 \tag{2}$$

Rewriting equation 1 and 2 in terms of the error produces:

$$e_1 = MOR - a_0 - a_1YS1 - a_2HS \tag{3}$$

$$e_2 = MOR - b_0 - b_1YS1 - b_2FHLB - b_3FSCA - b_4COMM - b_5DEP \tag{4}$$

Equations 3 and 4 may also be written in matrix form:

$$
\begin{vmatrix} e_1 & 1 \\ e_2 & 1 \end{vmatrix}
=
\begin{vmatrix} -a_1 & MOR \\ -b_1 & YS1 \end{vmatrix}
+
\begin{vmatrix} -a_0 & -a_2 & 0 & 0 & 0 & 0 \\ -b_0 & 0 & -b_2 & -b_3 & -b_4 & -b_5 \end{vmatrix}
\begin{vmatrix} 1 \\ HS \\ FHLB \\ FSCA \\ COMM \\ DEP \end{vmatrix}
$$

Placing the above in more general form produces:

$$u = B\,y + G\,x \tag{5}$$

In the reduced form equations, all endogenous variables are expressed in terms of the exogenous variables. Solving for y from 5 produces:

$$B\,y = -G\,x + u$$

$$y = -B^{-1}\,G\,x + B^{-1}\,u$$

If we let $-B^{-1}G = C$ *and* $B^{-1}u = v$, *then*

$$y = C\,x + v \tag{6}$$

Equation 6 may be expanded to produce the following reduced form equations.

$$MOR = c_{11} + c_{12}HS + c_{13}FHLB + c_{14}FSCA + c_{15}COMM + c_{16}DEP + v_1 \tag{7}$$

$$YS1 = c_{21} + c_{22}HS + c_{23}FHLB + c_{24}FSCA + c_{25}COMM + c_{26}DEP + v_2 \tag{8}$$

The reduced form coefficients and error terms are functions of the structural coefficients and error terms. For example:

$$c_{11} = \frac{(a_0 b_1 - a_1 b_0)}{a_1 - b_1} \text{ and } v_1 = \frac{(-b_1 e_1 + a_1 e_2)}{a_1 - b_1}$$

Appendix 3

Identification Issue

In matrix notation, the structural and reduced form equations may be stated as follows:

$$B \, y + G \, x = u \tag{1}$$

$$y = C \, x + v \tag{2}$$

Substituting for y from the reduced form expression, 2, into the structural equation, 1, produces:

$$B \, C \, x + B \, v + G \, x = u \tag{3}$$

Since $v = B^{-1} \, u$, and $B \, C \, x = -G \, x$, $B \, C = -G$.

Expanding $B \, C = -G$, multiplying out the matrices and solving for each c_{ij}, produces a series of identities for both the supply and demand equations.

demand	supply
$c_{11} = a_0 + a_1 c_{21}$	$c_{11} = b_0 + b_1 c_{21}$
$c_{12} = a_1 c_{22} + a_2$	$c_{12} = b_1 c_{22}$
$c_{13} + a_1 c_{23}$	$c_{13} = b_1 c_{23} + b_2$
$c_{14} = a_1 c_{24}$	$c_{14} = b_1 c_{24} + b_3$
$c_{15} = a_1 c_{25}$	$c_{15} = b_1 c_{25} + b_4$
$c_{16} = a_1 c_{26}$	$c_{16} = b_1 c_{26} + b_5$

For the demand equation, there are six equalities and three unknowns (a_0, a_1 and a_2), while for the supply equation, there are six equalities and six unknowns (b_0, b_1, b_2, b_3, b_4 and b_5). Thus, the demand equation is overidentified and the supply equation is exactly identified.

Notes

Chapter 1

1. Mutual savings banks usually purchase out-of-state loans through mortgage bankers.

2. Beginning in January 1981, savings and loans have additional discretionary power with respect to the composition of their assets and liabilities. The net effect is to make savings and loans more like commercial banks.

3. Kearl, Rosen and Swan (1975) review this literature.

4. Allan Meltzer is perhaps the most vocal critic of this view. See Meltzer (1974).

5. FNMA, GNMA and FHLMC respectively. Each agency has some common functions and each has some unique functions. See chapter 2.

6. See, for example, Jaffee and Rosen (1978) and Hendershott and Villani (1977).

Chapter 2

1. In 1930, savings and loan associations made about $1/3$ of residential mortgage loans. Source: Marvell (1969, p. 19).

2. While not significantly altering its responsibilities, the FHLBB was made a constituent agency of the Housing and Home Finance Agency by the 1947 Reorganization Plan (61 Stat. 954). However, Section 109 of the Housing Amendments of 1955 (69 Stat. 640) removed the Bank Board from HHFA and established it as an independent agency in the executive branch.

3. Source: *Federal Home Loan Bank Board Journal*, May 1981, p. 60.

4. In 1980 assessments accounted for over 83 percent of FHLBB income; employee compensation accounted for over 62 percent of expenses. Source: *FHLBB Annual Report*, 1980, p. 78.

5. Given the characteristics of FHLB securities, they are purchased by a broad segment of investors, both institutional and individual. In addition, legislation passed in 1969 authorized the Treasury to purchase up to $4 billion in FHLB securities when and if economic conditions warranted.

6. Of this total $12.6 billion were bonds (most with maturities of less than five years) and

$12.3 billion were discount notes (with maturities of one year or less). Source: *FHLBB Annual Report*, 1980, p. 84.

7. Source: *Federal Reserve Bulletin*, April 1983, p. A35.

8. This is not to say that all other FHLB programs and policies have little or no impact on credit availability. Kent (1981), for example, shows the impact of liquidity requirements on mortgage lending behavior by SLAs.

9. Source: 1982 *Savings and Loan Source Book*, p. 46.

10. Another important issue is the rate charged members versus the rate charged non-members. FHLBB regulations state that the rate charged non-members must be between ½ and 1 percent greater than the rate charged members (Section 525.25, FHLBB Regulations). The board may, however, suspend this regulation on a temporary basis if conditions warrant, which it did for part of 1974.

11. The 1932 Act discusses collateral in Section 10, paragraphs 1–4; FHLBB Regulations on collateral are found throughout Part 525.

12. Source: *FHLBB Annual Report*, 1980, pp. 104–06.

13. Source: *FHLBB Journal*, various issues.

14. During the first quarter of 1981, the net worth of all insured savings and loan associations declined by approximately $680 million. Source: *FHLBB Journal*, June 1981, p. 32.

15. Source: *FHLBB Annual Report*, 1970, p. 40.

16. Ibid., pp. 40–41.

17. Source: *FHLBB Annual Report*, 1974, p. 23.

18. Source: *FHLBB Annual Report*, 1980, p. 54.

19. The two criteria are:
    1. net worth to savings capital ratio of less than 2.5 percent (average for all SLAs as of 12/1980 was 6.5 percent)
    2. operating losses in at least three consecutive months
    Source: *FHLBB Annual Report*, 1980, p. 8.

20. This restriction was abolished in 1956.

21. Source: *Savings and Loan Fact Book*, 1979, p. 115.

22. Congress anticipated annual FNMA mortgage purchases would be between $400 and $450 million, and annual sales between $300 and $330 million. Thus, Congress expected FNMA's mortgage portfolio would be around $1 billion in 1964. See: *Hearings on S. 2938*, Senate Committee on Banking and Currency, 68th Congress, 2d Session, pp. 140–43.

23. Source: *FNMA Annual Report*, 1980, p. 19.

24. Ibid., p. 18.

25. Source: *Federal Reserve Bulletin*, various issues.

26. See: *Hearings on the Secondary Market Operations of FNMA and FHLMC*, Senate Committee on Banking and Currency, 94th Congress, 2d Session, p. 186.

27. Source: *FNMA Annual Report*, 1980, p. 15.

28. Ibid., p. 22.

29. Ibid., p. 17.

30. FNMA's chief executive officer, David Maxwell, expects FNMA to show a deficit for all of 1981. Source: *Wall Street Journal*, July 17, 1981, 2d section, p. 26.

31. This controversy was aired during Senate hearings before the Housing and Urban Affairs Subcommittee of the Committee on Banking, Housing and Urban Affairs, 94th Congress, 2d Session, held December 19, 1978. Much of the text presenting the contrasting views of HUD and FNMA is reprinted in the *1979 General Counsels' Conference Report*, published by FNMA.

32. Source: *GNMA Annual Report*, 1980, p. 20.

33. For a more detailed description of Ginnie Mae pass-through securities, see: Boykin (1979), pp. 214–16.

34. At the end of 1980, savings and loans held 16.4 percent of outstanding GNMA pass-throughs. Source: *GNMA Annual Report*, 1980, p. 9.

35. Ibid., p. 25.

36. Section 305, Emergency Home Finance Act.

37. Congress stated that the Corporation should not become merely a "dumping ground" for mortgages, but rather a true secondary market facility. The facility should be as much a seller, as well as a purchaser, of mortgages. See: *Senate Report No. 91-761*, Committee on Banking and Currency, 91st Congress, 2d Session.

38. As of December 31, 1979, savings and loans held 21.4% of outstanding PCs. Source: *The Mortgage Corporation Annual Report*, 1979, p. 7.

Chapter 3

1. See, for example, Grebler and Maisel (1963) and Kearl, Rosen and Swan (1975).

2. Schwartz (1970), Sparks (1967) and Swan (1970).

3. Kearl and Mishkin did find, however, that credit considerations appeared to be more important in explaining variation in multi-family housing starts than single family housing starts.

4. Additional evidence of the endogenous nature of FHLB and FSCA activity is provided Kaufman (1977).

5. Hendershott and Villani examined both FHLB and FNMA actions while Jaffee and Rosen examined only FSCA actions.

Chapter 4

1. Modifications are based on work by, Kearl and Rosen (1974), Silber (1973) and Swan (1972, 1973).

2. It is also possible to incorporate disequilibrium effects in the housing market. See, Swan (1972).

3. Some models of FHLB and FSCA behavior have used conditions in the mortgage market as the prime determinant of agency activity, rather than conditions in the housing market (e.g., Kearl & Rosen, 1974).

4. This simple scenario ignores changes in mortgage demand due to the initial increase in housing construction activity. As H increases, M^d shifts to the right. This shift, however, places upward pressure on the mortgage rate which depresses H.

5. Jaffee and Rosen define a rationing regime as one in which the mortgage rate rose by at least 5 basis points per month.

6. In both simulations, Jaffee and Rosen assume that agency commitments are taken down at the rate of $1 billion per month.

7. See for example, Silber (1970) and Kent (1981).

8. From 11.2% in 1965 to 16.1% in 1980.

9. Silber (1970) argues that, in a portfolio context, substitutes are most often of the same risk level. Complementary securities, on the other hand, are most often of different risk levels and thus, can be used to diversify a portfolio.

10. Demographic variables such as household formations and personal income may also affect mortgage demand. However, Rosen and Kearl (1974) suggest that demographic variables affect housing market activity which in turn affects mortgage market activity.

Chapter 5

1. Rao and Miller (1971) argue that the failure to adjust for significant seasonality may lead to biased and inconsistent regression coefficients.

2. See Rosen (1979) for a discussion of the patterns, causes and costs of seasonality in the housing and mortgage markets.

3. Schneeweis and Woolridge (1979) and Kmenta (1971) respectively discuss the major detection and correction techniques.

4. For a more detailed description of the X-11 iterative procedure, see: *The X-11 Variant of the Census Method II Seasonal Adjustment Program*, Technical Paper #15, U.S. Bureau of the Census (1967 Edition).

5. The trading day regression assumes, a priori, that all regression coefficients are equal to one. It tests this null hypothesis against the alternative that they are not equal to one.

6. The formulas used to calculate sum of squares are as follows:

$$SS\ (b/m) = \Sigma n_j\ (\overline{X}_j - M)^2$$
$$SS\ (w/m) = \Sigma\Sigma\ (X_{ij} - X_j)^2$$
$$SS\ (total) = \Sigma\Sigma\ (X_{ij} - M)^2$$

where n_j equals the number of observations in month j, $\overline{X}_j$ equals the mean S–I ratio for month j, M equals the grand mean, X_{ij} equals the S–I ratio for month j in year i.

7. The F test is based on the following assumptions:

1. $X_{ij} = \overline{X}_j + I_{ij}$.
2. $E(X_{ij}) = \overline{X}_j$.
3. $V(I_{ij}) = $ a constant, i.e. the irregular series is homoscedastic.
4. the irregular series is random.
5. the irregular series is normally distributed.

Chapter 6

1. See Black, et al. (1981), p. 464.

2. Identifying autoregressive processes, using ACF and PACF, is discussed by Nelson (1973), pp. 37–46. A more detailed discussion is in Box and Jenkins (1976), pp. 53–66.

3. The Durbin-Watson statistic is calculated as follows:

$$d = \frac{\Sigma(e_t - e_{t-1})^2}{\Sigma e_t^2}$$

where e_t are the residuals produced by OLS. The statistic tests $\rho = 0$, against the alternative $\rho \neq 0$.

4. For a specific definition of a simultaneous system of equations, see Kmenta (1971), p. 532.

Bibliography

Alberts, W. W. Business Cycles, Residential Construction Cycles and Mortgage Market. *Journal of Political Economy*, 1962, 263–81.

Arcelus, F. and Meltzer, A. H. The Markets for Housing and Housing Services. *Journal of Money, Credit and Banking*, 1973, 78–99.

Barth, J. R. and Bennet, J. T. Seasonal Variation in Interest Rates. *Review of Economics and Statistics*, 1975, 80–83.

Black, D. G., et al. The Impact of the GNMA Pass-Through Program on FHA Mortgage Costs. *Journal of Finance*, 1981, 457–69.

Boileau, W. A. GNMA Pass-Through: Overwhelming Success Story. *Mortgage Banker* (February), 1977, 20–99.

Box, G. E. P. and Jenkins, G. M. *Time Series Analysis: Forecasting Control* (Revised edition). San Francisco: Holden-Day, Inc., 1976.

Boykin, J. H. *Financing Real Estate*. Lexington, Mass.: Heath-Lexington, 1979.

Brady, E. A. A Sectoral Econometric Study of the Post-War Residential Housing Market. *Journal of Political Economy*, 1967, 147–58.

Cook, T. Q. The Residential Mortgage Market in Recent Years. *Economic Review*, Federal Reserve Bank of Richmond (September/October), 1974, 3–18.

——— and Hendershott, P. H. The Impact of Taxes, Risk and Relative Supplies on Interest Rate Differentials. *Journal of Finance*, 1978, 1173–86.

Dhrymes, P. J., and Taubman, P. J. An Empirical Analysis of the Savings and Loan Industry. *Study of the Savings and Loan Industry* (Vol. I). Washington: Federal Home Loan Bank Board, 1969.

Fair, R. C. *A Short Run Forecasting Model of the United States*. Lexington, Mass.: Lexington Books, 1971.

Ferri, M. G. An Empirical Examination of the Determinants of Bond Yield Spreads. *Financial Management* (Autumn) 1978, 40–46.

——— and Gaines, J. P. A Study of Yield Spreads in the Money Market: 1971–1978. *Financial Management* (Autumn) 1980, 52–59.

Garbade, K. D. and Hunt, J. F. Risk Premiums on Federal Agency Debt. *Journal of Finance*, 1978, 105–16.

Grebler, L. and Maisel, S. Determinants of Residential Construction: A Review of Present Knowledge. *Impacts of Monetary Policy*. Englewood Cliffs: Prentice-Hall, 1963.

Guttentage, J. The Short Cycle in Residential Construction, 1946–1959. *American Economic Review*, 1961, 275–98.

Hendershott, P. H. and Villani, K. The Federally Sponsored Credit Agencies: Their Behavior and Impact. *Capital Markets and the Housing Sector*, Buckley et al. (eds.). Cambridge: Ballinger Publishing Company, 1977.

Huang, D. S. The Short-Run Flows of Non-Farm Residential Mortgage Credit. *Econometrica*, 1966, 433–59.

———. Effects of Different Credit Policies on Housing Demand. *Study of the Savings and Loan Industry* (Vol. III). Washington: Federal Home Loan Bank Board, 1969.

Jaffee, D. M. An Econometric Model of the Mortage Market. *Savings Deposits, Mortgages and Residential Construction*, Gramlich and Jaffee (eds.). Lexington: Heath-Lexington, 1972.

———. Cyclical Variations in the Risk Structure of Interest Rates. *Journal of Monetary Economics*, 1975, 309–25.

——— and Rosen, K. T. Estimates of the Effectiveness of Stabilization Policies for the Mortgage and Housing Markets. *Journal of Finance*, 1978, 933–46.

Kaufman, H. M. An Analysis of the Behavior of Federal Mortgage Market Agencies. *Journal of Money, Credit & Banking*, 1977, 349–55.

Kearl, J. R. and Mishkin, F. S. Illiquidity, the Demand for Residential Housing and Monetary Policy. *Journal of Finance*, 1977, 1571–86.

———, Rosen, K. and Swan, C. Relationships between Mortgage Instrument, the Demand for Housing and Mortgage Credit: A Review of Empirical Studies. *New Mortgage Designs for Stable Housing in an Inflationary Environment*, Modigliani and Lessand (eds.). Conference Series No. 14, Federal Reserve Bank of Boston, 1975.

Kent, R. J. An Analysis of Countercyclical Policies of the FHLBB. *Journal of Finance*, 1981, 61–80.

Kmenta, J. *Elements of Econometrics*. New York: Macmillan, 1971.

Maisel, S. J. A Theory of Fluctuations in Residential Construction Starts. *American Economic Review*, 1963, 359–83.

———. Non-business Construction. *The Brookings Quarterly Econometric Model of the United States*. Chicago: Rand McNally Co., 1965.

———. The Effects on Monetary Policy on Expenditures in Specific Sectors of the Economy. *Journal of Political Economy*, 1968, 796–814.

Marvell, T. B. *The Federal Home Loan Bank Board*. New York: Praeger, 1969.

Meltzer, A. H. Credit Availability and Economic Decisions: Some Evidence from the Housing and Mortgage Markets. *Journal of Finance*, 1974, 763–77.

Moore, G. H. and Shishkin, J. *Indicators of Business Expansion and Contractions*. New York: National Bureau of Economic Research, 1967.

Myers, J. L. *Fundamentals of Experimental Design* (3rd edition). Boston: Allyn and Bacon, 1979.

Nelson, C. R. *Applied Time Series Analysis*. San Francisco: Holden-Day, 1973.

Rao, P. and Miller, R. *Applied Econometrics*. Belmont, California: Wadsworth Publishing Company, 1971.

Rosen, H. S. and Rosen, K. T. Federal Taxes and Home Ownership: Evidence from Time Series. *Journal of Political Economy*, 1980, 59–75.

Rosen, K. T. *Seasonal Cycles in the Housing Market*. Cambridge: The MIT Press, 1979.

——— and Bloom, D. E. A Microeconomic Model of Federal Home Loan Mortgage Corporation Activity. *Journal of Finance*, 1980, 959–72.

——— and Kearl, J. *A Model of Housing Starts, Mortgage Flows and the Behavior of FHLBB and FNMA*. Working paper No. 27, MIT-Harvard Joint Urban Studies Center, 1974.

Schneeweis, T. and Woolridge, J. R. Capital Market Seasonality: The Case of Bond Returns. *Journal of Financial and Quantitative Analysis*, 1980, 939–58.

Schwartz, H. The Role of Government-Sponsored Intermediaries in the Mortgage Market. *Housing and Monetary Policy*. Boston: Federal Reserve Bank of Boston, 1970.

Seiders, D. F. *The GNMA-Guaranteed Pass-Through Security*. Staff Study No. 108, Board of Governors of the Federal Reserve System, 1979.

Silber, W. *Portfolio Behavior of Financial Institutions*. New York: Holt, Rinehart and Winston, 1970.

————. A Model of Federal Home Loan Bank System and Federal National Mortgage Association Behavior. *Review of Economics and Statistics*, 1973, 308–20.

Sparks, G. R. An Econometric Analysis of the Role of Financial Intermediaries in Post-War Residential Building Cycles. *Determinants of Investment Behavior*. New York: National Bureau of Economic Research, 1967.

Swan, C. Homebuilding: A Review of Experience. *Brookings Papers on Economic Activity*, 1970, 48–70.

————. *A Quarterly Model of Housing Starts: A Disequilibrium Approach*. Working Paper No. 39, Federal Home Loan Bank Board, 1972.

————. *A General Equilibrium Model of FHLB and FNMA Actions*. Working Paper #44, Federal Home Loan Bank Board, 1973.

————. The Markets for Housing and Housing Services: A Comment. *Journal of Money, Credit and Banking*, 1973, 960–72.

Wachtel, P. *GNMA Securities and the Portfolio Behavior of Mutual Savings Banks*. Working Paper No. 230, Salomon Brothers Center, New York University, 1981.

Index

Author Index